WHAT IS THE TRUTH?

WHAT IS THE TRUTH?
A FARMYARD FABLE FOR THE YOUNG
TED HUGHES

DRAWINGS BY R.J. LLOYD

faber and faber

LONDON · BOSTON

First published in 1984
by Faber and Faber Limited
3 Queen Square London WC1N 3AU

Printed in Great Britain by
Redwood Burn Ltd, Trowbridge, Wiltshire.

British Library Cataloguing in Publication Data

Hughes, Ted
What is the truth?
I. Title   II. Lloyd, R.J.
821'.914   PR6058.U37

ISBN 0–571–13155–7

by Ted Hughes

The Hawk in the Rain
Lupercal
Wodwo
Selected Poems (*with Thom Gunn*)
Crow: From the Life and Songs of the Crow
Cave Birds: An Alchemical Cave Drama
Gaudete
Remains of Elmet
Moortown
Selected Poems 1957–1967
River

Seneca's Oedipus (*adapted by Ted Hughes*)

for children
Season Songs
Under the North Star
The Earth-Owl and Other Moon-People
The Iron Man: A Story in Five Nights
Meet My Folks
Nessie the Mannerless Monster
How the Whale Became
The Coming of the Kings and other plays

edited by Ted Hughes
Poetry in the Making: An anthology of Poems and
    Programmes from *Listening and Writing*
A Choice of Emily Dickinson's Verse
A Choice of Shakespeare's Verse
The Rattle Bag (*with Seamus Heaney*)

For Clare and Michael

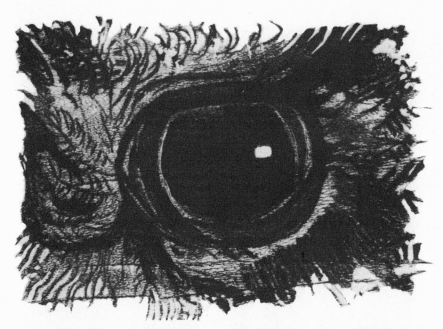

ONE DAY GOD'S SON
LOOKED DOWN AT THE EARTH

and said to his Father: "I would like to go down and visit mankind."

And God said: "Why would you want to do that?"

And God's Son answered: "It might be interesting. I'm curious. I might learn something."

"Stay here," said God. "Curiosity is dangerous. Be satisfied with Heaven."

But God's Son still went on gazing at the earth. He didn't quite know why, but something about mankind fascinated him. It puzzled him, and disturbed him, but it fascinated him.

"I really would like to visit mankind," He said. "It looks quite exciting. Besides, travel broadens the mind."

God put his arm round his Son's shoulders.

"Take my advice," said God. "Stay here. Mankind cannot teach you anything. Mankind thinks it knows everything. It knows everything but the Truth."

God's Son frowned. What did his Father mean? How could mankind be so clever, and yet so ignorant, at the same time? How could it know everything, and yet not know the Truth?

God watched his Son's baffled face. And He decided the time had come for a memorable lesson.

So God took his Son's hand and led him down to earth. It was night, about two o'clock in the morning, when their feet touched the top of a grassy hill, and God's Son felt his feet wet with the dew. Mankind was asleep. God's Son stood with wide eyes, and all around him he saw the valleys in mist, and the sleeping farms, under the full moon. And away below he could see the spire and roofs of a village, in a hollow, in the moonlit mist.

"We will speak to the people," said God. "We will ask them a few simple questions. Then you shall hear. In their sleep, they will say what they truly know. That is another odd thing about mankind. When they are awake, they are deepest asleep. When they are asleep, they are widest awake. Strange creatures!"

And God said: "To begin with, let us ask the Farmer a question." And God called to the Farmer.

The Farmer was snoring into his pillow, huddled on his side, with his knees tucked up and his arms folded, under a mound of blankets. His snore made the bed vibrate. His short hair stuck out in all directions. In his sleep, he still seemed to be working with all his strength. Beside him, face upwards, his wife seemed to be singing a thin high note, with her eyes closed in the purity of the sound, though in fact she was hardly breathing at all. A tiny little bird breath now and again. Moonlight heaped over their bed like a drift of snow.

Then in his sleep the Farmer heard the voice of God. And his soul left his body where it lay, and flew to the hilltop, where God and his Son sat on a log under the full moon.

And God said to the Farmer: "Tell us about one of the creatures on your farm."

9

10

The Farmer stared at God in blank astonishment. The two figures glowed, golden red. They were almost transparent, as red-hot metal seems to be almost transparent. He recognized that log. It was the trunk of a fir-tree that had blown down last winter. He had trimmed it only a week ago, where it lay between two oak-trees. He wasn't sure yet how he would use it, but it was a good log, and as he gazed at the two men he wondered if they might be scorching the wood where they sat.

"Tell us," suggested God, "about the creature you last thought of."

Back on his bed, the Farmer's body had suddenly stopped snoring and for a moment even stopped breathing. Then he heaved on to his back. The dream, where he had been sorting giant partridges in the cattle pens in his big building, seemed to have all flown away. And out on the hilltop, under the moon, his misty soul—slightly lit by the glow from the figures in front of him—began to sing to God:

A grand bird is the Partridge, a wild weed of a sort.
The cheapest weed on all my ground, it never costs a thought.
And when it puffs and flies it's Bang! and Bang! and pretty sport.

I love to see them racing on their bumpy little wheels
And hear their rusty axles twisting out their creaks and squeals—
They're plumping up the sweetest, whitest meat of all my meals.

A son of the soil the Partridge is, from earth-clods he was born.
I love to see him crane his neck up, out of the young, green corn.
And better than bottled beer and skittles when the stubble's shorn

I love it when a covey Whoosh! explodes with such a rattle
And every bit spins whizzing and it's Bang! and Bang! a battle,
And dinner comes tumbling out of the air! Better than bedding cattle!

12

"Remember that," said God to his Son. And as the Farmer's soul sank to the grass, looking like a woolly rosy sheep, God spoke to the Farmer's son.

The boy's shape lay rolled in a patchwork quilt. The parts of a half-assembled model space-ship lay scattered about the floor. He himself was floating through the stars in his pyjamas, his arms spread wide.

But as God spoke he found himself on the hilltop, with his feet in the grass, beside his father, while two glowing creatures, sitting like men on a log in front of him, were looking at him, and one of them was saying:

"Tell us about the creature you think about the most."

"You mean Bess," said the boy. And as he spoke, his eyes glowed, reflecting the brightness of the two strange beings.

Bess my badger grew up
In a petshop in Leicester. Moony mask
Behind mesh. Dim eyes
Baffled by people. Customers cuddled her,

Tickled her belly, tamed her—her wildness
Got no exercise. Her power-tools,
Her miniature grizzly-bear feet,
Feet like little garden-forks, had to be satisfied

Being just feet,
Trudging to-fro, to-fro, in her tight cage,
Her nose brushed by the mesh, this way, that way,
All night, every night, keeping pace

With the badgers out in the woods. She was
Learning to be a prisoner. She was perfecting
Being a prisoner. She was a prisoner. Till a girl
Bought her, to free her, and sold her to me.

What's the opposite of taming? I'm unteaching
Her tameness. First, I shut her in a stable.

But she liked being tame. That night, as every night,
At a bare patch of wall the length of her cage
To-fro, to-fro, she wore at the wood with her nose,
Practising her prison shuffle, her jail walk.

All day, dozing in the gloom, she waited for me.
Every supper-time, all she wanted was
Me to be a badger, and romp with her in the straw.
She laughed—a chuckling sort of snarl, a rattle,

And grabbed my toe in my shoe, and held it, hard,
Then rolled on to her back to be tickled.
"Be wild," I told her. "Be a proper badger."
She twisted on to her feet, as if she agreed

And listened. Her head lifted—like a hand
Shaped to cast a snake's head shadow on the wall—
What she'd heard was a car. She waddled away
Shawled in her trailing cape of grey feathers,

And looked back. Sniffed a corner. Listened.

I could see she was lonely.

A few nights later
Her claws went wild. And they tunnelled
From stable to stable, connecting four stables.

Then bored up through the wall so the long loft
Became her look-out. After that,
If shouting in the yard, or a tractor, disturbed her,
You'd see her peering down through the dusty panes,

And if the loft door had been blown open
She'd poke her face out, furious, then slam it.
Soon she'd quarried out through the back of the stables
And with about three cartloads of stony rubble

From under the stables, she landscaped her porchway—
And the world was hers. Now, nightly,
Whatever she can shift, she'll shift, or topple,
For the worm, the beetle, or the woodlouse beneath it.

She tasted clematis roots, and now she's an addict.
She corkscrews holes in the wet lawn with her nose,
Nipping out the lobworms. With her mine-detector
Finds all the flower-bulbs. Early workmen meet her

Plodding, bowlegged, home through the village.

Already she hardly needs me. Will she forget me?
Sometimes I leave black-treacle sandwiches,
A treat at her entrance, just to remind her—
She's our houseproud lodger, deepening her rooms.

Or are we her lodgers? To her
Our farm-buildings are her wild jumble of caves,
Infested by big monkeys. And she puts up with us—
Big noisy monkeys, addicted to diesel and daylight.

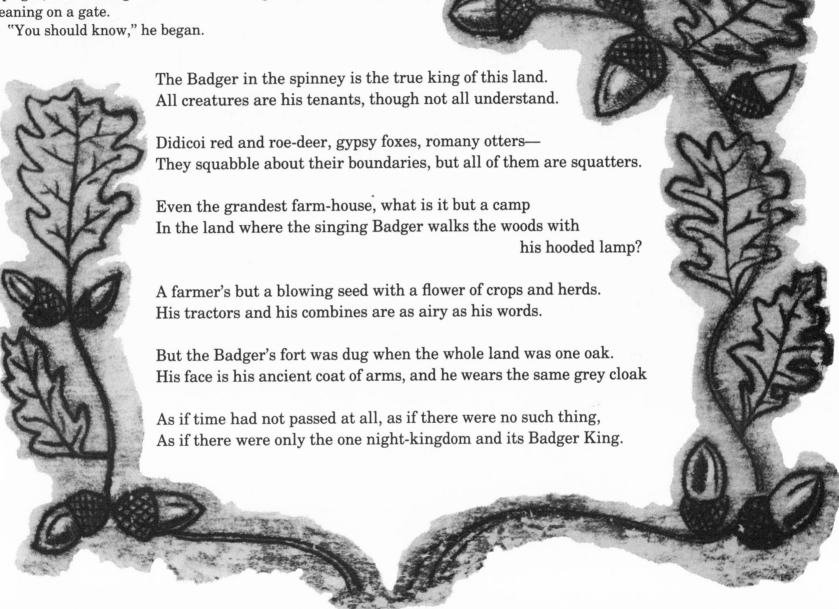

The Farmer rose up from the grass. He rose lightly, like a balloon, and floated, about a foot above the grass, not quite upright, but leaning towards the two figures, as if he were leaning on a gate.

"You should know," he began.

The Badger in the spinney is the true king of this land.
All creatures are his tenants, though not all understand.

Didicoi red and roe-deer, gypsy foxes, romany otters—
They squabble about their boundaries, but all of them are squatters.

Even the grandest farm-house, what is it but a camp
In the land where the singing Badger walks the woods with
his hooded lamp?

A farmer's but a blowing seed with a flower of crops and herds.
His tractors and his combines are as airy as his words.

But the Badger's fort was dug when the whole land was one oak.
His face is his ancient coat of arms, and he wears the same grey cloak

As if time had not passed at all, as if there were no such thing,
As if there were only the one night-kingdom and its Badger King.

"I'd like to see one of these badgers," said God's Son.

But God was calling the Farmer's daughter.

The Farmer's daughter lay pillowed in her hair. At this moment she was dreaming she was a horse. She was galloping through the world, bringing the news to all the horses of the world that a new foal had been born, a magic foal, and she laughed in her sleep as she galloped. And it was true, a new foal had been born on the farm, that day.

But then in her dream, as she galloped over the dusty Mongolian plains, shouting her news to the dark, stirring lakes of wild horses, she heard the voice of God calling to her, saying:

"Tell us about it."

And in a moment she was no longer a galloping horse. She was herself, standing on the hill above the farm. And she saw her father and brother lying there mistily in the grass, their chins propped on their hands, gazing up at two radiant figures who sat on a log. She knew at once they were God and his Son, and she began to tell them about that new foal.

Yesterday he was nowhere to be found
In the skies or under the skies.

Suddenly he's here—a warm heap
Of ashes and embers, fondled by small draughts.

A star dived from outer space—flared
And burned out in the straw.
Now something is stirring in the smoulder.
We call it a foal.

Still stunned
He has no idea where he is.
His eyes, dew-dusky, explore gloom walls and a glare doorspace.
Is this the world?
It puzzles him. It is a great numbness.

He pulls himself together, getting used to the weight of things
And to that tall horse nudging him, and to this straw.

18

He rests
From the first blank shock of light, the empty daze
Of the questions—
What has happened? What am I?

His ears keep on asking, gingerly.

But his legs are impatient,
Recovering from so long being nothing
They are restless with ideas, they start to try a few out,
Angling this way and that,
Feeling for leverage, learning fast—

And suddenly he's up

And stretching—a giant hand
Strokes him from nose to heel
Perfecting his outline, as he tightens
The knot of himself.
                            Now he comes teetering
Over the weird earth. His nose
Downy and magnetic, draws him, incredulous,
Towards his mother. And the world is warm
And careful and gentle. Touch by touch
Everything fits him together.

Soon he'll be almost a horse.
He wants only to be Horse,
Pretending each day more and more Horse

Till he's perfect Horse. Then unearthly Horse
Will surge through him, weightless, a spinning of flame
Under sudden gusts,

It will coil his eyeball and his heel
In a single terror—like the awe
Between lightning and thunderclap.

And curve his neck, like a sea-monster emerging
Among foam,

And fling the new moons through his stormy banner,
And the full moons and the dark moons.

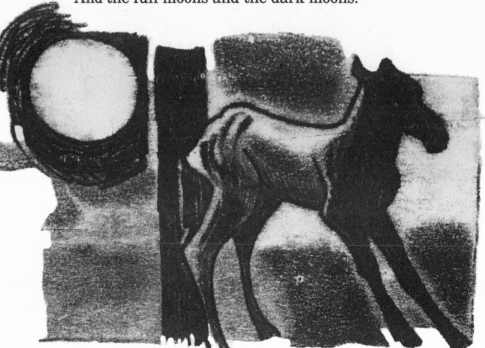

19

20

"That sounds like a fine beast" said God's Son. "Even if it isn't a badger."

"It isn't the Truth either," said God. "Neither the whole Truth nor half the Truth. Even so, it's closer to the Truth than her father or her brother."

"So how is that?" asked God's Son.

"Listen to the girl's mother," said God.

The Farmer's wife, in bed beside the sleeping shape of her husband, had not stirred. She still seemed to be singing, in that angelic choir, an everlasting top note. Her hair was clamped in curlers, so that her head looked like a Rolls-Royce aircraft engine. Tomorrow would be market day, her day out. She was dreaming she stood at the table, kneading dough, when suddenly a mouse pulled at the hem of her long grandmotherly dress. And she heard the voice of God saying:

"Tell us about the cow."

In a moment she stood on the hill. She stared at the two glowing men, or the creatures that seemed to her to be men. And she still seemed to be singing that soundless top note, only now it was surprise.

Back in her bed, her shape had closed its mouth, smacked its lips, and smiled. Then her shape on the hilltop spoke:

There's comfort in the Cow, my dear, she's mother to us all.
When Adam was a helpless babe, no mother heard him call.
The Moon saw him forsaken and she let a white star fall.

Beasts sharpened their noses when his cry came on the air.
Did a she-wolf nurse him with the wolf-cubs in her lair?
Or cuffed among rough bear-cubs was he suckled by a bear?

21

No, the gentle Cow came, with her queenly, stately tread,
Swinging her dripping udder, and she licked his face and head,
And ever since that moment on the Cow's love he has fed.

A man is but a bare baboon, with starlit frightened eyes.
As earth rolls into night he cheers himself with monkey cries
And wraps his head in dreams, but his lonely spirit flies

To sleep among the cattle in the warm breath of the herd.
Among the giant mothers, he lies without a word.
In timeless peace they chew their cuds, till the first bird

Lifts the earth back into the clock, the spirit back into the man.
But the herd stays in Paradise, where everything began,
Where the rivers are rivers of foaming milk and the eyes are African.

God slapped his knee. "Nearly!" he exclaimed. "Nearly!"
God's Son frowned. He couldn't see what his Father meant.
But before he could ask, the Farmer rose from where he lay. As
his wife sank down in a rosy mist, coming to rest gently, with
her elbows in the grass, and her chin in her hands, gazing with
shining eyes at the glowing men, he rose straight up and
began to sing, loud, as if he had a pint glass of ale in his hand.

The Cow is but a bagpipe,
All bag, all bones, all blort.
They bawl me out of bed at dawn
And never give a thought
     a thought
They never give a thought.

The milk-herd is a factory:
Milk, meat, butter, cheese.
You think these come in rivers? O
The slurry comes in seas
     seas
The slurry comes in seas.

A cowclap is an honest job,
A black meringue for the flies.
But when the sea of slurry spills
Your shining river dies
     dies
Your shining river dies.

Say this about cows:
Nothing can stop
From one end the Moo
From t'other the flop
    flop
    flop
    flippety-flop

Floppety-flippety.

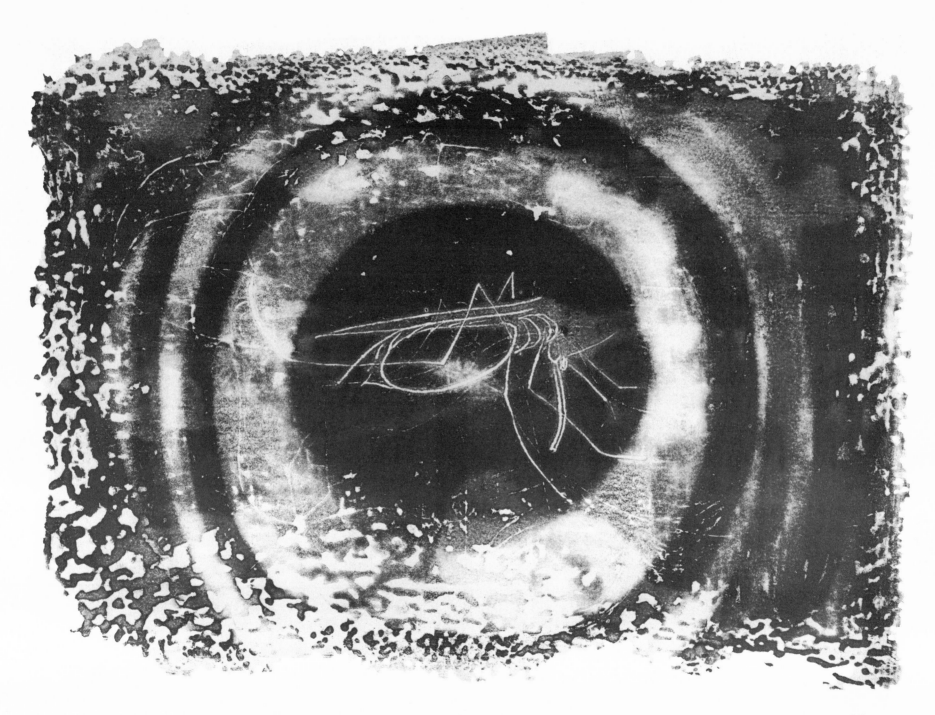

24

But as he sank back, his daughter was already speaking. She had somehow guessed that these two angelic beings on the log were giving them an examination, and when she saw the old bearded one shaking his head sadly she knew her father had made a mistake. So straight away she began:

I think
There's a summer ocean liner in cows—
Majestic and far off,
With a quiet mysterious delight,
Fading through the blue afternoon.

And there's a ruined holy city
In a herd of lying down, cud-chewing cows—
Noses raised, eyes nearly closed
They are fragments of temples—even their outlines
Still at an angle unearthly.
As if a ray from heaven still rested across their brows,
As if they felt it, a last ray.

And now they come, swinging their ballast, bowing
As if they dragged slow loads slightly uphill,
There's a dance in the swaying walk of cows

With their long dancers' necks, to left and to right
And that slight outfling of hooves, a slow dance-step—
Bodies of oil,
Dancers coming from hard labour in the fields.

And there's a flare of wide skirts when they swirl
On such exact feet
With the ankles of tall dancers

In under the girders and asbestos.

The Farmer too seemed to realize that his song about the Cows hadn't been quite right. He felt he must make amends.

"Farming's never been the same," he said, "since we lost the horses."

"But you have a horse," said God's Son. "It's just had a foal."

"Ah!" sighed the Farmer. "Not like the old horses!"

"Tell us," said God's Son.

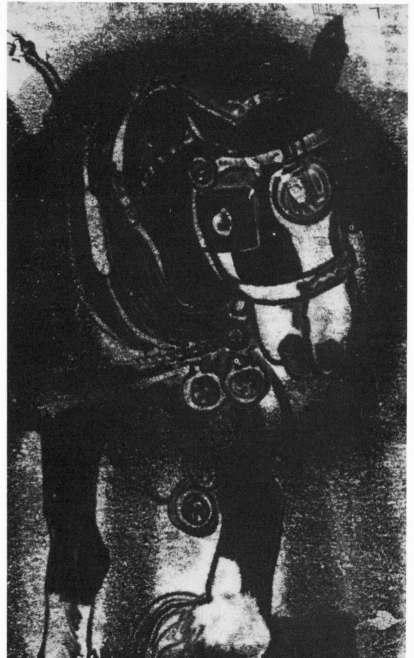

One time we had nothing else of course and handsome they were.
We have a picture of our old horses, like a blurred pair
Of Victorian Grandads, in their beards and fobs, at a Country Fair.

You'd never believe the elastic in them, their nimbleness and their power.
Though they'd look like whispy old haystacks, propped-up and leaning there,
They could earth-quake like flood-water, brown-backed and tossing over a weir.

Every road and yard reeked of horses, they were everywhere.
Hard to credit it now. I sometimes dream I'm back there, my stare
Sunk in the wave that lifts and sprawls aside from the plough-share.

It's like a dream of riding the boughs of a windy, working tree,
An oak that rips the live ground open, tearing its tap-root free.
My horses are great, creaking boughs. And all I seem to see

Is their huge, plum-tight haunches revolving, heavily, like mill-wheels.
Watery quake-weights. Wading the earth, like old shaggy angels.
I'd gaze into their furnace glow and go in a daze for miles.

Our last friendly angels—that's what they were.
Their toil was a kind of worship, their every step a bowing of prayer
Hidden under tangled hair and sweat. But the tractor shoved them all

Straight back to God. It didn't take much to undo them.
They were made of the stuff of souls, and the little grey Ferguson rattled straight through them.
Now you will not see them. But I saw them.

28

His daughter watched the two on the log. She could see they seemed to like her father's old horses. But that last part seemed a bit rough, the horses being shoved back to God by tractors. She knew that wasn't what they wanted to hear, and she bit her lip. But her brother was speaking.

"Let me tell you about our Galloway calf without a tail," he said. "It looked like a woolly black bear. It was born in the snow and its tail froze and broke—"

"That's enough," interrupted the Farmer. "We don't want to hear about such things."

He'd sooner tell God about the cow that bore triplets. But he wasn't sure about that either, because one of them had been a poor little thing and a friend of his had asked him with a laugh if it was a new type of rat.

Then God's Son said: "I expect you have lots of cats."

"Only one that's any good," said the Farmer. "The rats have them outclassed."

"Rats!" said God firmly. "What about rats?"

As God spoke, a misty globe rose from the village below and came speeding towards the hilltop.

"Sing the Rat!" A wild voice echoed over the treetops.

Down in the village, the Poacher, who by day was an odd-job man among the farms, let out a groan and twisted in his chair, where he had fallen asleep fully dressed beside his Rayburn stove. He had meant to wake at 1 a.m. and go to the rabbity hill with his nets and ferrets. But sleep held him fast. And here he was, at three o'clock, floating as a spirit before God and his Son, with his mouth wide open, and shouting to the whole hushed landscape:

Sing the hole's plume, the rafter's cockade
Who melts from the eye-corner, the soft squealer
Pointed at both ends, who chews through lead

Sing the scholarly meek face
Of the penniless Rat
Who studies all night
To inherit the house

Sing the riff-raff of the roof-space, who dance till dawn
Sluts in silk, sharpers with sleek moustaches
Dancing the cog-roll, the belly-bounce, the trundle

Sing the tireless hands
Of the hardworking Rat
Who demolishes the crust, and does not fail
To sign the spilt flour.

The Rat the Rat the Ratatatat
The house's poltergeist, shaped like a shuttle
Who longs to join the family

Sing his bright face, cross-eyed with eagerness
His pin fingers, that seem too small for the job
Sing his split nose, that looks so sore
O sing his fearless ears, the listener in the wall

Let him jump on your head, let him cling there
Save him from sticks and stones

Sing the Rat so poor he thrives on poison
Who has nothing to give to the trap, though it gapes for a year
Except his children
Who prays only to the ferret
"Forget me" and to the terrier
"In every million of me, spare two"

Who stuffs his velvet purse, in hurry and fear
With the memory of the fork,
The reflections of the spoons, the hope of the knives
Who woos his wife with caperings, who thinks deep

Who is the slave of two fangs

O sing
The long-tailed grey worry of the night hours
Who always watches and waits
Like a wart on the nose
Even while you snore

O sing
Little Jesus in the wilderness
Carrying the sins of the house
Into every dish, the hated one

O sing
Scupper-tyke, whip-lobber
Smutty-guts, pot-goblin
Garret-whacker, rick-lark
Sump-swab, cupboard-adder
Bobby-robin, knacker-knocker
Sneak-nicker, sprinty-dinty
Pintle-bum

"Was that a case of everything but the Truth?" asked God's Son.
"If you want some Truth," said the Farmer, "let me tell you about one of your birds."
"A complaint?" cried God, frowning.

With his clothes-peg beak and his bald face
The Rook tramples all over my place.

He's no beauty. His face is actually
A sort of bleached callus, all scaly

Worn with plunging his beak up to the peepers
Down between earth-clods for crawlers and creepers.

He also pulls up the seed those creatures clutch
Just as it's starting to sprout—and that is such

Vandalism I go with my gun.
Seventy rooks whirl up but down comes one.

31

So now he'll swing from a stick and with both arms
Signpost his tribe to move on, to different farms.

   The Farmer's son could hardly wait for the Farmer to finish,
before he started:

Rooks love excitement. When I walked in under the rookery
A gale churned the silvery, muscular boughs of the beeches, and the wet leaves streamed—
It was like a big sea heaving through wreckage—

And the whole crew of rooks lifted off with a shout and floated clear.
I could see the oiled lights in their waterproofs
As the blue spilled them this way and that, and their cries stormed.

Were they shouting at me? What did they fear?
It sounded
More like a packed football stadium, at the shock of a longed-for goal—

A sudden upfling of everything, a surfing cheer.

The Farmer's soul seemed to think he might have gone a bit too far, insulting God's rooks. He stood up very straight, and he held the tips of his thumb and of the middle finger of his left hand lightly together, slightly raised, as if he were about to throw a dart. But no, he was singing. He wasn't singing in his pint of ale voice. He was singing in his Sunday parlour at the piano voice, so that his wife gazed at him with her shining eyes, very much as she had been gazing at God. And he sang:

The Fox is a jolly farmer and we farm the same land.
He's a hardworking farmer, with a farmer's hard hand.

In the corn he farms hares—and what wallopers he rears!
And he plans his poultry system while a-feeling their ears.

In the pond he farms ducks, and a few Christmas geese.
He's an eye for their meat, for their down, for their grease.

In the hayfield it's marvellous the flocks of his voles
And everywhere in the hedges fat rats in their holes.

And everywhere in the hedges, partridges lay clutches
Of eggs for his collection, and some he lets hatch. He's

A hardworking farmer and we farm the same ground.
In our copse he tills rabbits worth many a pound,

And sometimes a catch-crop of squawking young crows.
In the old wood it's beetles he lifts with his nose.

And out on the pasture he borrows my rams,
And my pedigree ewes, for his pedigree lambs.

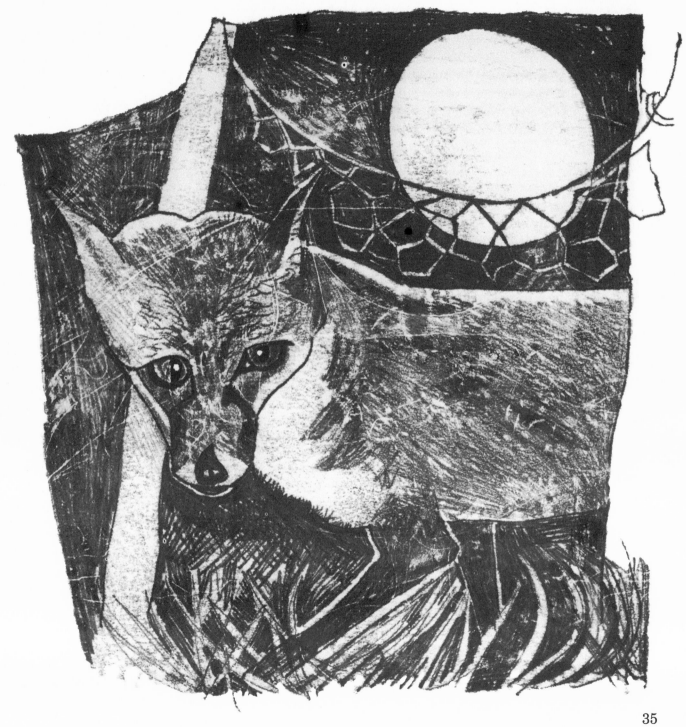

"Very nice for the Fox," said God. "But I wonder what the lambs think of it."

"Yes," cried God's Son. "What about the lamb?"

In a cottage on the other side of the hill, under a clump of tall holly trees, a bedroom was loud with snores. The snorer lay flat on his back, his arms flung wide, his big nose jutting up in the moonlight. It was the Shepherd. And he wasn't dreaming at all. He was too tired. But when he heard the voice of God calling: "Tell us about the Lamb," he dived out through his window like a swallow and found himself on the hilltop, in front of the glowing men.

He felt very startled. Still dog-tired after shearing all day, the last thing he wanted to do was talk about lambs and sheep. But the eyes of the glowing men compelled him.

Back on his bed, his body stopped snoring. It groaned once, and was silent.

And the Shepherd's soul began:

The problem about lambs
Is that each lamb
Is a different jigsaw—and each piece
Is a different problem.

Getting born—one problem
Of many little pieces. The Lamb has to solve it
In the dark, with four fingers.

Once he's born—it's a case
Of which problem comes first. His mother won't have him.
Or he's deficient and won't cooperate.
Or he gets joint-ill
Which sneaks in through the little wick of his umbilical cord before it dries up—

Arthritis for infants.

After that comes Orf—known as Lewer.
Ulcers of the nose, of the lips, of the eyes, of the toes,
All at once,
As you read about in the Bible.

Awful things waiting for lambs.

As he grows
Just trotting about gives him footrot. That is, his hooves fall apart
Exactly like rotten mussels,
And the cure is to cut them back to the quick and the blood
With a knife.

His fleece is for Scab. For Ticks. For Keds. And for Itch-mites.
If God gave the sheep her fleece
Why didn't he clean it? Well, I have to clean it
And a right job it is.

Everything makes him cough. Just plain eating
Gives him Fluke. Who invented the Fluke?
It looks like the Fluke of an anchor.
Where was God dozing when he let the Fluke
Anchor in the Lamb?

Then his back end for maggots.
The blow-fly is Beelzebub. Maggots are his imps.
God I think forgot sheep altogether.

Sheep is a cruel puzzle of problems.

Brain—what looks just like brainlessness
Is a one-track genius
For roaming, for searching out new pastures,
Always somebody else's,

For unravelling weak places in hedges
And producing a fine clear gap
With a deep trench of tramplings going straight through it.

Sheep is a machine
Of problems
For turning the Shepherd grey as a sheep.

God's Son interrupted the Shepherd.
"Now you've unloaded your worries and your complaints," he said, "tell us about the Sheep."

God smiled and nodded. The Shepherd seemed surprised. He didn't know he had anything more to say. Plenty more complaints. But God was watching him, and suddenly he had an idea:

40

If the world were a Sheep, would the Sheep be its Lamb?
The Sheep is a soft sort of rock
For moonlight and sunlight and rain
Quarried from the world's sheepishness.

The Sheep is a small inland sea,
A wave on four legs,
A living foam, with a heart for a fish
And blood of real sea-water, and half-moon eyes.

The Sheep is a mobile heaven, it nibbles the hill,
A manageable cloud,
A cloud for a lawn, or a field-corner.
A small, patient cloud
In whose shade the Shepherd's dog can rest.
A cloud going nowhere,
Growing on the hillside, fading from it—
A cloud who teaches quiet.

And the Lamb is a flower—
A flower of the snow.
Fearing nothing, like a flake of the snow
That falls on the Iceberg,

And loving the tops of everything, just like the snow,
Dreadful crags and ledges, just like the snow,
Yet loving the sun, too.
A warm flower, an armful of blossom.

And inside the warm lamb-flower
Is a whole constellation
Of stars of water

And the cry of the lamb-flower, such a melting cry,
Is its dark root
In its cloud mother

Who looks like an old ewe.

"Very nice," said God. "But is it the Truth?"
The Shepherd sighed. He'd done his best, and he'd surprised himself. He'd quite enjoyed it. But now suddenly he felt very sleepy. He looked down at the Farmer and his wife, their son and daughter, and there of all people the Poacher too, all lying in the grass, chins on their hands, gazing at God and his Son, and he felt like lying down among them. But God's powerful eyes were still on him. And so he said, rather wearily:

The Truth about the Sheep alas
Is that it leads a childish life
Head in the fairy-tale of grass
And never thinks about the knife.

They leap when shearers shave them bare.
"Look, we're lambs again," they bleat.
But their lambs lament and stare
"First you were wool but now you're meat!"

Heavy harvests on the trot
Bags of cash that sit in clover
Where would Sheep be if they were not?
Sheep would long ago be over.

God frowned. He did not seem to like what He heard, and He looked at his Son uneasily. But his Son was speaking: "Why don't we call the Vicar? Surely he'll get things right. He's the Shepherd of a flock too."

Even as God's Son spoke, a faint light rose from the tip of the church steeple, as if it had come out of the weathercock, or as if it were the brass polished weathercock itself, now flying towards the hill, gleaming in the moon. But the weathercock was still there, gleaming on the steeple. And as the little flame came towards them they could see that it was inside a glassy form, like the flame inside the glass chimney of a paraffin lamp. And they all heard the Vicar's unmistakable voice:

The beggarly Bat, a cut out, scattily
Begs at the lamp's light
A lit moth-mote.

What wraps his shivers?
Scraps of moon cloth
Snatched off cold rivers.

Scissored bits
Of the moon's fashion-crazes
Are his disguises
And wrap up his fits—

For the jittery bat's
Determined to burst
Into day, like the sun

But he never gets past
The dawn's black posts

As long as night lasts
The shuttlecock Bat
Is battered about
By the rackets of ghosts.

He sank to the grass beside the Farmer's wife and everybody was silent. God and his Son stared at the Vicar, who stared back, blinking nervously, and clutching the grass tightly, as if he felt he might float away and be lost. He still thought this was a dream.

Then the Poacher, who had rolled on to his side to gaze at the Vicar, smiled and spoke: "Quickness comes from the Devil, like the bat from the belfry. Slowness comes from God. Now Buzzard is slow.

Big hands—broad, workaday hands.
Are they darkened with working the land?
When does he work?
Whoever saw him do anything?

Most of the day he elongates a telephone pole
With his lighthouse look-out and swivel noddle—
He looks more like a moth, crawled up there, owlish,
A furry night-creature of lichen,
Dazed by the sun and wind, clinging and waiting.

Or you see him sitting mid-field
Always doing nothing.
Listening to tangled tales by mole and by bee
And by soft-headed dandelion.

Or he mooches along the old hedgebanks,
Flap-rags, unemployable,
A bit touched in the head. Sometimes
By pure chance he steps on a baby rabbit—
Then he looks like an old Granny
Trying to get her knickers off.
                              O beggared eagle!
O down-and-out falcon! Up!
Let's see you up there—up! Up!
That's better!
                    Now let your flags unfurl,
Mew at the sun—give us that eagle feeling!

He floats,
Or he swims—a very slow butterfly-stroke,
Stretching up for the blue. But so lazy!

Finally, he just lets the sky
Bend and hold him aloft by his wing-tips.

There he hangs, dozing off in his hammock.

Mother earth reaches up for him gently.

"A riddle!" said the Farmer's son suddenly. Everybody
looked at him. And God and his Son looked at him.

Who
Wears the smartest evening dress in England?
Checks his watch by the stars
And hurries, white-scarfed,
To the opera
In the flea-ridden hen-house

Where he will conduct the orchestra?

Who
With a Robin Hood mask over his eyes
Meets King Pheasant the Magnificent
And with silent laughter
Shakes all the gold out of his robes
Then carries him bodily home
Over his shoulder,
A swag-bag?

45

And who
Flinging back his Dracula cloak
And letting one fang wink in the moonlight
Lifts off his top hat
Shows us the moon through the bottom of it
Then brings out of it, in a flourish of feathers,

The gander we locked up at sunset?

"A fox!" cried God's Son, and clapped his hands, gripping his fingers together. He seemed delighted. But seeing God shake his head, the Farmer's daughter called out: "Hear about our pigs!"

"Tell about the bees," said the Farmer. "Tell about sweet things. What's a pig but a pig?"

"A pig," said his daughter sharply, "is anything but a pig. And no pig is ever really happy either."

"Why is that?" asked God.

The Pig that ploughs the orchard with her nose
Returns
Strutting in her tiny tutu.

The Pig that lies unearthed out there, a giant potato,
Or snores in the straw, an eyeless, legless
Water-bed of wobble and quake,
Can sprint faster than you can.

The sow fallen out there, cratered in mud,
Like the circus fat lady
Fallen off her tightrope, is not happy.
She wants to be a real lady.

The Pig that peers up at you, with blubbery nose
And eyes red from weeping
Wants to be you.

47

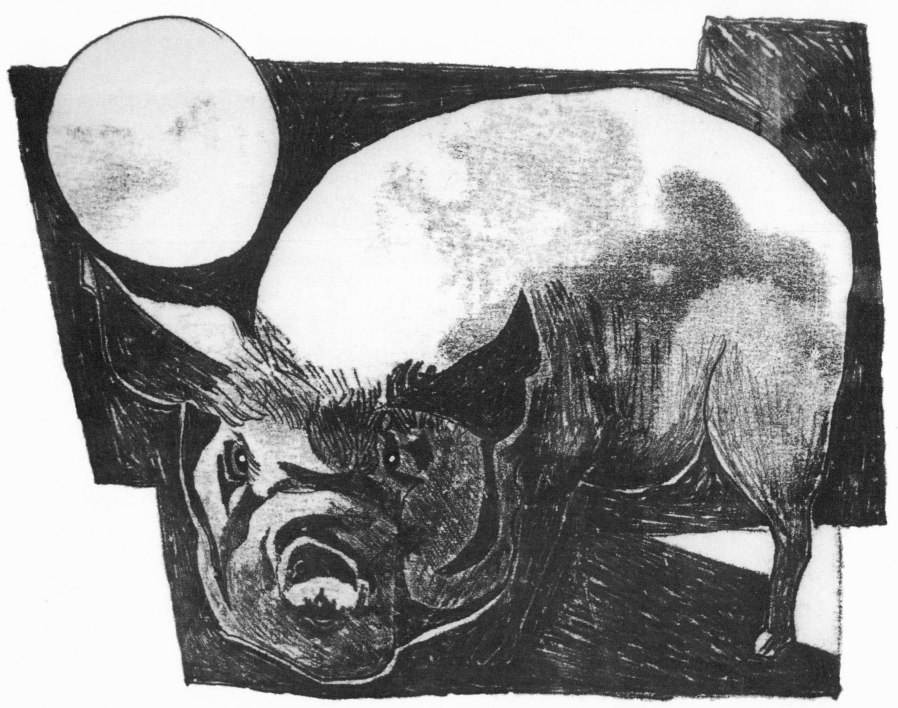

48

And the lean weaner, with his sawn-off shotgun grin,
Squints his little Judas eye at you.
Oh he's wicked! He burps laughter!
A flea
Earthquakes the world of pig.
And he's splitting at the seams
To keep in the explosion of laughter.
His eyelids screw down tight, keeping it in.
He wants to be a naughty comedian.

The big boar has problems
With the battered swill-buckets of his ears.
He keeps trying to arrange them over his eyes
Like big poppy petals, but they're too floppy.
I know I'm no beauty, he says. I live for my children.

And the piglets, in elevens and thirteens,
Galloping like apples poured from a barrel,
Flogging themselves with their ears,
Trying to escape from their tails
Cry: Take us with you, take us with you.

All pine for the day they will be people.

"When a pig drinks, what bird does it next?" asked the
Farmer's son.
    "Swallows!" shouted God's Son, delighted.
And the Shepherd suddenly woke, from where he'd been
nodding, as if he'd heard his name called, and rising slowly
from the grass, he began:

Blue splinters of queer metal are swallows,
Magnetized along weird lines of magnetic force—
So they go,
Slide along, hardly a wing-beat, sparkling.

Not mad like swifts. Flight like writing,
Foreign sort of sky-writing—Arabic—
A scrolling, swirling sort of hand—
Everything a signature and a flourish.

There's a heat-wave in swallows—
Dry static of the baked air crackling
Off their wing-tips, and no let-up, round and
Round and round the sun-struck dizzy buildings.

49

50

There's thunder too in swallows.
Glitter-dark, flickering over the white hay
Where the flies hide from the lightning
When the air tightens, and the whole sky sags low like a big, warm drop.

And the Farmer's wife went straight on:

What is loveliest about swallows
Is the moment they come,
The moment they dip in, and are suddenly there.

For months you just never thought about them
Then suddenly you see one swimming maybe out there
Over our bare tossing orchard, in a slattery April blow,
Probably among big sloppy snowflakes.

And there it is—the first swallow,
Flung and frail—like a midge caught in the waterskin
On the weir's brink—and straightaway you lose it.
You just got a glimpse of whisker and frailty.

Then there's nothing but jostled daffodils, like the girls running in from a downpour
Shrieking and giggling and shivering,
And the puckered primrose posies, and the wet grit.
It's only a moment, only a flicker, easy to miss—

That first swallow just swinging in your eye-corner
Like a mote in the wind-smart,
A swallow pinned on a roller of air that roars and snatches it away
Out of sight, and booms in the bare wood

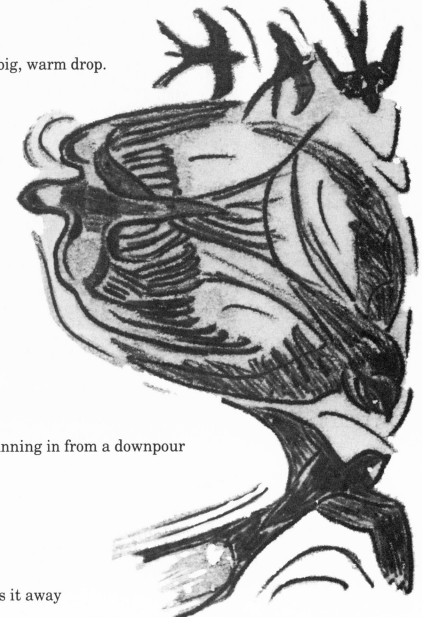

And you know there'll be colder nights yet
And worse days and you think
"If he's here, there must be flies for him,"
And you think of the flies and their thin limbs in that cold.

The Vicar coughed softly, so everybody looked at him. It was clear he was going to say something serious. He had relaxed a little. His hands were now flat on the ground—still ready to clutch at the roots of the grass, but not clutching. He seemed to be looking at God over the tops of his spectacles, and so he would have been if they had not been lying folded on the table beside his bed. And now he spoke.

I agree
There's nothing verminous, or pestilential, about swallows.
Swallows are the aristocrats
The thoroughbreds of summer.
Still, there is something sinister about them.
I think it's their futuristic design.
The whole evolution of aircraft
Has been to resemble swallows more and more closely.
None of that putt-putting biplane business
Of partridges and pheasants,
Or even the spitfire heroics of hawks.
When I was a boy I remember
Their shapes always alarmed me, slightly,
With the thought of the wars to come,
The speed beyond sound, the molten forms.
You might say
They have a chirruppy chicken-sweet expression,
With goo-goo starlet wide-apart eyes,

And their bills seem tiny, almost retroussé cute—
In fact, the whole face opens
Like a jet engine.

And before this, they solved the problem, did they not,
Of the harpoon.

53

Without moving from where he reclined, with his cheek resting on his hand, the Farmer spoke, in his usual way, so they all knew it was the end of the argument.

I'll say this for swallows, they're marvellous workers.
You think they're sunning by the pond—but No!
They're down there gathering balls of mud—in their mouths!
They're building their huts with their beaks!

You see them looping all the directions of the compass
Into a floral bow, and all day
It looks like skater's truant play. It is not.
It's full-tilt, all-out labour, stoking their nestful.

You'd think they'd play a bit, after, with their family—
All figure-flying together. No—they stick at it.
Brood after brood—right up to Michaelmas
The crib's a quiverful of hungry arrows.

They must go round the whole globe twenty times
Just among my buildings. Marvellous!
The truest, keenest, bluest blade-metal,
Whetted on air, every move smoother—

The finest tool on the farm!

"Swifts" said the Poacher, "sleep thousands of feet up. You see them coming down in the early dawn, you hear them while they're still out of sight."
"All birds sleep in God," said the Vicar solemnly.
"Led there by the Magpie," said the Poacher. "In surplice and cassock."

"A donkey's more religious," said the Farmer's son. "And he's no sort of colour."

"What is religious about a donkey?" asked God's Son.

"My donkey," began the Farmer's daughter:

My donkey
Is an ancient colour. He's the colour
Of a prehistoric desert
Where great prehistoric suns have sunk and burned out
To a blueish powder.

He stood there through it all, head hanging.

He's the colour
Of a hearth-full of ashes, next morning,
Tinged with rusty pink.

Or the colour of a cast-iron donkey, roasted in a bonfire,
And still standing there after it, cooling,
Pale with ashes and oxides.

He's been through a lot.

But here he is in the nettles, under the chestnut leaves,
With his surprising legs,
Such useful ready legs, so light and active,

And neat round hooves, for putting down just anywhere,
Ready to start out again this minute scrambling all over Tibet!

And his quite small body, tough and tight and useful,
Like traveller's luggage,
A thing specially made for hard use, with no trimmings,
Nearly ugly. Made to outlast its owner.

His face is what I like.
And his head, much too big for his body—a toy head,
A great, rabbit-eared, pantomime head,
And his friendly rabbit face,
His big, friendly, humourous eyes—which can
                              turn wicked,
Long and devilish, when he lays his ears back.

But mostly he's comical—and that's what I like.
I like the joke he seems.
Always just about to tell me. And the laugh,
The rusty, pump-house engine that cranks up
                              laughter
From some long-ago, far-off, laughter-less desert—

The dry, hideous guffaw
That makes his great teeth nearly fall out.

"There's a story about that laugh," said God. "Who knows that story?"

"I know a story," said the Shepherd, "about the crowing of the Cock."

"First," said God's Son, "tell the story about the cooing of the Dove."

"Ring-doves?" The Farmer almost shouted. "Wood pigeons?" And he turned to God, saying:

Pigeons! They're problems. You know why their crop's
                                                called a crop?
It's where my harvest goes, goes, goes without stop.

Pudgy pests! Prime pods packed with my profit!
They pitch on my farm only for what they pinch off it.

Proper piratical poachers! And what do they pay?
A splintery pigeon pie at the end of the day.

"The holiest bird of all!" said the Vicar. "What an end!"

"They can't compare with the Honey-bee," said the Poacher, "for wing-work and religion."

"What about the Bee is it that's so devout?" asked God.

At a big wedding
The bees are busy.
Everywhere there are bridesmaids
Almost brides.

And the air
All round the May hive
Twangs
Dangerously. Missiles.

Gingery gleams
Aslant through the ashpoles—
Telegrams
Coming in.

The bees fall
On to their knees, and humbly head-down crawl
Into their crammed church
Where they are fattening

With the earth's root-sweetness
A pale idol, many-breasted,
Made of wax. The One
Who'll make their swarm immortal.

The orchard is dizzy with bells.
Everything is tearful. The fumbling, mumbling
Priestly bee, in a shower of petals,
Glues Bride and Groom together with honey.

"Badgers love honey," said the Farmer's son.
And the Poacher started again. He was getting warmed up.

Main thing about badgers is hating daylight.
Funny kind of chap snores all day
In his black hole—sort of root
A ball of roots a potato or a bulb maybe
A whiskery bulb he loves bulbs he'll do a lot to get
                              a good bulb
Worms beetles things full of night
Keeping himself filled up with night
A big beetle wobbling along nose down in the mould
Heavy weight of night in him
Heavy pudding of night solid in him
                              and incredibly heavy
Soaking out through his beetle-black legs
Leaving the hair-tips on his bristly back drained empty
And white and his face drained stark-white
A ghost mask really a fright mask
                              I know night-shift miners
Are very pale but he's whitewashed

Like a sprout's white I suppose underground
He sprouts his nose slowly
Surprising to see it sticking out of the ground
To sniff if the sun's gone—soon he comes rolling out
A fat bulb with a sniffing sprout, a grey mushroom
Just bulging out of the ground and sitting there
                              on top of it
Scratching his fleas sniffing for stars

His sniffing around is a bit like a maggot

Then he's off following his sniff
With his burglar's mask on and his crowbar
Under his moonlight cloak
And all night he's breaking and entering
Deadlogs wasps' nests hedgehogs, old wild man of
                              the woods in his woad
Crashing about, humming to himself

Amazing physique he has Eskimo wrestler
Really like a Troll bristly gristly
Armpits like an orangoutang when you examine him
And a ridge on his skull like a gorilla
Packed in muscle a crash-helmet of muscle
His head is actually one terrific muscle
With a shocking chomp and sleepy little eyes
To make it seem harmless. But he's harmless enough
Even if he acts guilty. And he makes you smile
When you see his back-end bobbing along in the
                              dawn-dew
With the sack of himself bouncing on his gallop
Just like a sack of loot. My Dad said
Kill a badger kill your granny. Kill a badger never see
The moon in your sleep. And so it is.
They disappear under their hill but they work a lot
                              inside people.

Unnoticed by all except God and his Son, another misty woolly soul-shape had joined them. He sat slightly off to one side, cross-legged, as if he were listening to them all, but meant to take no part. It was the Schoolteacher. And now he suddenly spoke.

"The Treecreeper" he said, "is easily overlooked." And he went on:

On a tree-bole, a zig-zag upward rivulet
Is a dodgy bird, a midget ace
Busy as a shrew, moth-modest as lichen.

Inchmeal medical examination
Of the tree's skin. Snapshot micro-scanner
And a bill of instant hypodermic.

He's unzipping the tree-bole
For more intimate scrutiny. It sticks. Jerks.
No microbe dare be, nor bubble spider.

All the trees are waiting, pale, undressed,
So he can't dawdle. He jabs, dabs, checks essentials,
Magnet-safe on undersides, then swings

In a blur of tiny machinery
To the next patient's foot, and trickles upwards,
Murmuring "Good, good!" and "Good, good!"

Into the huge, satisfying mass of work.

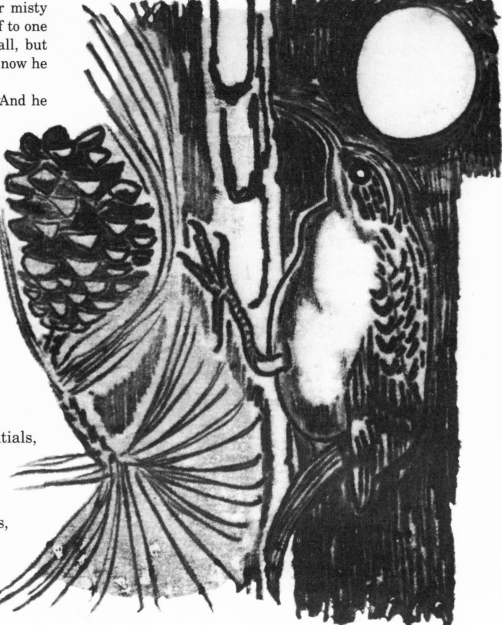

64

Everybody was silent. Even God seemed to be thinking.
Then they all realized the Poacher was muttering something.
It sounded almost like a song. And as they listened he raised
his voice:

The Weasel whizzes through the woods, he sizzles through the brambles.
Compared to him a rabbit hobbles and a whippet ambles.

He's all the heads of here and there, he spins you in a dither,
He's peering out of everywhere, his ten tails hither thither.

The Weasel never waits to wonder what it is he's after.
It's butchery he wants, and BLOOD, and merry belly laughter.

That's all, that's all, it's no good thinking he's a darling creature.
Weight for weight he's twice a tiger, which he'd like to teach you.

A lucky thing we're giants! It can't be very nice
Dodging from the Weasel down the mazes of the mice.

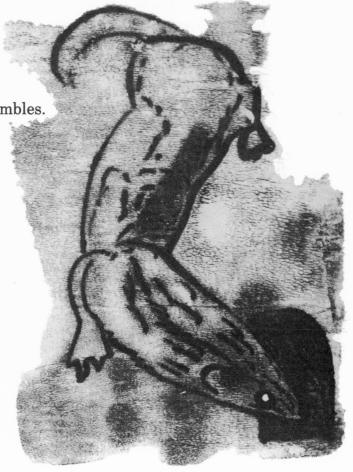

And then God's Son asked: "What's happened to the Truth?
Are we getting any Truth yet?"

God smiled and looked at the Schoolteacher. "Can you give
us the Truth about those mice?" He asked.

The Schoolteacher frowned. Then he began, and as he spoke,
in his measured way, he stuck out first his thumb, then his
forefinger, then his middle finger, and so on, as he counted off
the points about the Mouse.

65

The Mouse's round and round and abouts
Bind the whole farm secretly together.
The cat brings in the bitten knots of the string.

The Mouse's sweet look, so intense
Like a young prodigy
Girl violinist, raises the tone of the parlour.

The Mouse in the kitchen, bouncing ping-pong
Among footballing boots, dumb with panic
Lets the silly skirts do the squealing.

While the family sleeps like sacks of turnips
The Mouse, trembling, pop-eyed, solitary,
Braves the ghost.

The Mouse who has watched from his crannies
Everybody's secret and told nobody,
Steals all night with a good conscience.

They all looked at God, who was stroking his beard, and
nodding slightly, not in approval, but as if He had just under-
stood something about the Schoolteacher. And suddenly,
taking them all by surprise, God's great arm shot out. His
long, bony forefinger stuck out like a pistol barrel, straight at
the Farmer, who stared back at Him in alarm.

"Mice," said God.

The Farmer eased himself on to one elbow and frowned
slightly. He didn't like it at all when God was stern. But after a
while he began:

Mice are funny little creatures

                                     you nearly don't see them

Getting out so fast under the sacks more like a bird's shadow

Amazing living like that on fearful lightning

Funny too how they smell like lions did you ever smell lions in a zoo?

You see one come tottering out
When maybe you're just sitting quiet and he'll come right out
With his nose-end wriggling investigating
Every speck of air he seems to be—high on his trembly legs
Very long legs really and his queer little pink hands
Little monkey's hands very human I always think
And his wiry bent tail high up there behind him
Wavering about he looks to be on a tightrope

Then he finds something and starts trembling over it
His nibbling is an all over trembling, his whole body
Trembles as if he were starving and couldn't wait
But it's really listening, he's listening for danger—so sensitive
He's trembling it's like a tenderness
So many things can hurt him
And his ears thin as warm wax you've squeezed between your finger and thumb
Always remind me of an elephant's ears
A bit shapeless and his long face really like an elephant
If he had a trunk he'd be a tiny elephant exact
At least his face would and his tail being a kind of trunk at the wrong end
And his feet being so opposite to great elephant's feet
Help remind you of elephants altogether he really is like an elephant
Except his size of course but that reminds you of elephants too
Because it's the opposite end of the animals
Like they say extremes meet I can understand
Why mice frighten elephants but they're dear little things
I don't mind what they nibble

"There's somebody knows the house even better," said the Farmer's son.

"Who's that?" asked God's Son.

"The Spider," cried the Farmer's daughter.

"The Fly," said the Farmer's son.

The Fly
Is the Sanitary Inspector. He detects every speck
With his Geiger counter.
Detects it, then inspects it
Through his multiple spectacles. You see him everywhere
Bent over his microscope.

He costs nothing, needs no special attention,
Just gets on with the job, totting up the dirt.

All he needs is a lick of sugar
Maybe a dab of meat—
Which is fuel for his apparatus.
We never miss what he asks for. He can manage
With so little you can't even tell
Whether he's taken it.

In his black boiler suit, with his gas-mask,
His oxygen pack,
His crampons,
He can get anywhere, explore any wreckage,
Find the lost—

Whatever dies—just leave it to him.
He'll move in
With his team of gentle undertakers,
In their pneumatic protective clothing, afraid of nothing,
Little white Michelin men,
They hoover up the rot, the stink, and the goo.
He'll leave you the bones and the feathers—souvenirs
Dry-clean as dead sticks in the summer dust.

Panicky people misunderstand him—
Blitz at him with nerve-gas puff-guns,
Blot him up with swatters.

He knows he gets filthy.
He knows his job is dangerous, wading in the drains
Under cows' tails, in pigs' eye-corners
And between the leaky broken toes
Of the farm buildings—
He too has to cope with the microbes.
He too wishes he had some other job.

But this is his duty.
Just let him be. Let him rest on the wall there,
Scrubbing the back of his neck. This is his rest-minute.

Once he's clean, he's a gem.

A freshly barbered sultan, royally armoured
In dusky rainbow metals.

A knight on a dark horse.

70

The Farmer shook his head, saying:

I don't know about flies.

I don't like to see a fly
Wandering about in the air
Outside a rabbit-hole, then going in.
Somebody's died down there.

I don't like to see a fly
Tapping the eye ball
And peering into the eye
Of a cow stretched out in its stall.

Every creature in its own way
Mistakes the Weasel
For somebody else—too late.

And I hate to feel a fly
When I'm taking a snooze after lunch
Walk to my mouth-corner—
As if just checking a hunch.

The Weasel's white chest
Is the pretty pinafore of the waitress
Who brings the field-vole knife and fork.

The Weasel's black ripe eyes
Brim with a heady elderberry wine
That makes the Rat drunk.

"How's that for Truth?" asked God's Son, looking at his
Father. He wasn't sure he liked the sound of that Fly.
    But the Poacher answered, saying: "I know a Truth, but I
dare say it's a bit of a lie."
    God and his Son looked at the Poacher as he spoke:

The Weasel's fully-fashioned coat,
Lion-colour, wins her admittance
To the club of snobby goslings.

When the Weasel dances her belly dance
Brainless young buck rabbits
Simpering, go weak at the knees.

When the Weasel laughs
Even the Mole sees the joke
And rolls in the aisles, helpless.

And hardly pausing for breath, the Poacher suddenly burst
into song:

O the White-collared Dove has a swollen nose!
His head is nipped thin for his eyes are too close.
And the blood in his eye is as pink as his toes!

He stopped abruptly and looked at the Vicar. But it was the
Farmer's daughter who went on with:

He has an acrobatic stunt—in April
He bounces up an invisible rigging in the air
And with a toppling clap of his wings
Launches off at the top, like a wide-armed
                                        free-fall diver.

Sometimes he goes up so steep and crazy
Clapping his wings at the height he almost
Comes over backwards.

That makes his betrothed go hot and cold.

She's watching from the ash. He corkscrews down
To breathe in her ear—

His throat is plummy,
Some peacock on his nape,
A ruffle of silks—a rippling

It's the flame inside there, playing on the metals,
The voice in there, the muffled bellows
That swells the oaks, that splits the chestnut's wrappers—

There are bells in the blue haze and soft brass bands
At a Sunday distance, but only wood pigeons
Breathe on the embers that make summer simmer—

"Who woos? Both of us,"
Or "Who woos? You do,"
Or just "Who woos—me—"

The weathercock melts.

"Now for the story behind the weathercock!" cried God's
Son.
    "The Cock, the Cock, the common Cock," said the Shepherd,
testily. "The Rooster."
    He paused a moment, then began:

Why is it
The roustabout Rooster, raging at the dawn
Wakes us so early?

A warrior-king is on fire!
His armour is all crooked daggers and scimitars
And it's shivering red-hot—with rage!

And he screams out through his megaphone:
"Give me back my Queens!"

What's happened?

He fell asleep, a King of Tropic India
With ten thousand concubines, each one
Gorgeous as a volcanic sunset—

But now he wakes, turned inside out—a rooster!
With eleven flea-bitten hens!

And he remembers it all. No wonder he screeches:
"Give me back my Queens!"

No wonder his scarlet cheeks vibrate like a trumpet!

But it's no use. He seems to droop.
It's simply no use.
All that majestic armour is just feathers.

But now it comes over him again!
Again he goes all stiff—and quivering!
He aims himself at the sun.
He looks like a flame-thrower,
And with one blast, as if it were his last,
Tries to turn himself back outside in
With: "Give me back my Queens!"

The sun yawns and saunters away among some clouds.
The empty-headed hens
Are happy unriddling the cinders.

Only the cockerel dreams and trembles and flames.

God's Son clasped his knees tightly with pleasure. "If that's not the Truth," He said to his Father, "is it at all like it?"

"It contains" said his Father, "one grain of Truth. A grain of Truth fallen among cinders."

"Then a hen will soon find it," said the Vicar. And he went on:

> The Hen
> Worships the dust. She finds God everywhere.
> Everywhere she finds his jewels.
> And she does not care
> What the cabbage thinks.
>
> She has forgotten flight
> Because she has interpreted happily
> Her recurrent dream
> Of clashing cleavers, of hot ovens,
> And of the little pen-knife blade
> Splitting her palate.
> She flaps her wings, like shallow egg-baskets,
> To show her contempt
> For those who live on escape
> And a future of empty sky.
>
> She rakes, with noble, tireless foot,
> The treasury of the dirt,
> And clucks with the mechanical alarm clock
> She chose instead of song
> When the Creator
> Separated the Workers and the Singers.

77

With her eye on reward
She tilts her head religiously
At the most practical angle
Which reveals to her
That the fox is a country superstition,
That her eggs have made man her slave
And that the heavens, for all their threatening,
Have not yet fallen.

And she is stern. Her eye is fierce—blood
(That weakness) is punished instantly.
She is a hard bronze of uprightness.
And indulges herself in nothing
Except to swoon a little, a delicious slight swoon,
One eye closed, just before sleep,
Conjuring the odour of tarragon.

"My goat" said the Poacher, "has a kind of fragrance."
"Goats!" exclaimed the Farmer's wife. "The worst of all
garden pests!" And she went on:

A few quick flirts of their shameless tails—
Each tail looks like a whiskery woodlouse
Jerking to attention—and every rose fails.

And their triangular, axe-shaped, munching heads
Seem to say—looking at me cock-eyed—
Funny, your young apple trees have all just died.

A plague out of the Old Testament are goats!
Satan, sitting in their throats,
Looks at me through their evil eyes and gloats.

When a goat pulls at your coat, it's a sampling bite.
There it stands, chewing its marble, thinking:
I'll gnaw this whole globe down to a meteorite!

"The Goat" said the Schoolteacher, "is definitely not a
religious beast. Or at least it's not a godfearing beast."
"Oh?" said God. "Why not?"
And the Schoolteacher said:

With a watery trickle of hooves, a tender bleating,
Nose to the grindstone, working at eating,
Round the Mediterranean Sea
With all his family
The Billy Goat passed
Like a nuclear blast.

Out of the dusty fall of Babylon the Great
Walked the Goat, still searching for something to eat.

Out of the tombs of Egypt stepped forth
The Goat, chewing a scrap of mummy cloth.

Into the cave, from which Christ's body had flown,
The Goat peered, evil-eyed, with his horns on.

St. Columba's High School,
Dunfermline.

Whenever a goat stops eating
And aims at you with his nose
Remember the deserts waiting
Between his dirty toes.

"The Goat" said the Poacher, "was one half of the great god Pan."
"Is that true or false?" asked God's Son, looking at his Father.
And the Poacher said:

If the Goat's eye really were a globe
            all of pale, iceberg-haunted sea,
If the Goat's eye really were the tip of an icicle
            forming in a cold rusty furnace,
If the Goat's eye really had moved, suddenly,
            in the face of the statue of a stone god
            dug up in a desert

Though the Goat's dainty lips
            are a kind of dryish sea-anemone
Though the Goat's mean lips
            are the leaves of a thorn on a blustery headland

And though the Goat's front legs
            are the ballet of spray flung higher up the cliff
            seeming to cling there
            while it nibbles the buds
And though the Goat's hooves are
            the first rattle of the stones on your coffin

And though the Goat's hairs truly are
            fallen from a constellation
            a stray greasy starlight, radioactive with chaos
Into the milking bowl

The Nanny Goat's milk is still the sweetest of milks

And her cheese of cheeses

82

"If I'm going to have my garden stripped," said the Farmer's
wife, "I'd prefer my geese to have the benefit of it."
"Is there any Truth in a goose?" asked God's Son.
And the Farmer's wife said:

Geese are godly creatures, not just for Christmas show.
At my first note on their bucket, though it's ten degrees below,
Their choir stands in a ring and they lift their throats of snow.

And they carol out their discords, till their tall necks fence me in
With a rusty-shipyard bonging echoing hollow din.
Noël, Noël, they clang to God, which can't be called a sin.

Devil's feet of lizard leather! Wrangling, squirmy necks!
Hissing cauldrons! Haggish witches gabbling out a hex!
It's only the gander warning you from his wives with a threat of pecks—

The ladies laugh their loony laughter, gossiping together,
Or arguing about a puddle, or a duck's feather.
Or they remember the white seas and the snows of polar weather

And all begin to sing, and stretch up as if to fly
At a sudden vision of icebergs, and they yodel out a cry
That cannons between iron mountains and an iron sky—

But all fall like snow. It is sad, but it must be.
I sit and bare the breast of down, the weight across my knee,
And I'm ankle-deep in the whiteness, and the fluff goes floating free,

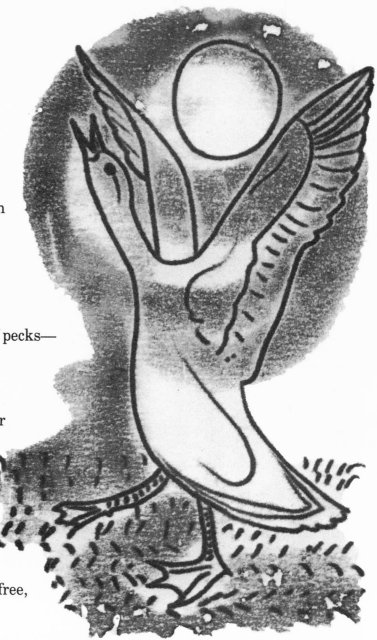

Till the poor body's nude as a babe, except for the neck and head,
The neck in its muff, its ruff of plumes, pretending to be dead,
But the bright eye still open hearing every word that's said,

And the beak that worked so hard at the world, and sang to me so strong,
Holding carefully silent the plump tip of its tongue
Lest it spoil our Christmas Feast with any whisper of wrong.

"Do you disagree with something?" ask God quietly. He had seen the schoolteacher smiling and shaking his head. The Schoolteacher stopped smiling at once. But then after a moment he said:

I remember two geese—mainly remember
The muck they waddled in—you wouldn't dare
Tread there, under sad apple trees.
Two dirty queens, hating each other.

They couldn't fly to the ice-floes. Did they ever see snow fuming
Off sun-dazzle peaks? Their necks had long lost
The poured cream of a goose's plump neck softness.
Instead, clutching their draggly bunched-up skirts,

Lifting out of mud bare feet that were
More like rubber frogfeet, these two queens
Held their noses high—blue eyes always
Peering over something—or bowed, studying

Mud for another egg. Bub, bub, bub!
Nowhere to put their load of dirty laundry,
Each foot going down like a paint-brush—sploodge!
Sploodge!—wobble weighty,

Not quite tripping up at each step,
Sagging their keels. A toppling pyramid
Of sixty or more
Mudded, rain-cold, probably rotten eggs,

Under the wall, was the addled castle
Each of them seemed to be trying to own.
Odd eggs lay everywhere—cannonballs
Of their miserable battle—abandoned

Where they'd rolled. Though these geese were queens,
That was a prison yard, and they were convicts,
And their punishment was to go on laying eggs
And to go on stealing each other's eggs

And never know they were spellbound. It was April.
Sunlight peered through the wall.
One jabbed at a muddy stub-end of cabbage.
One sat back in the armchair of herself,

A little smoke of down stirred in her nostril.

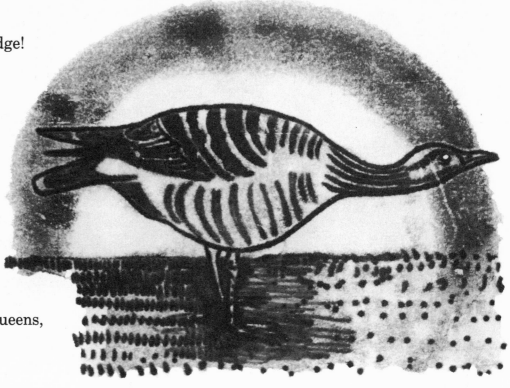

"Dreadful to have to pick your living out of the mud," said the Poacher.

"Or to get it creeping about the hedges like a Jenny Wren," said the Farmer, with a hard look at the Poacher.

"Or hanging upside down like a bluetit," said the Farmer's son.

"Or sticking your nose in the bog, right up to the eye-corners, like a snipe," said the Farmer's wife.

"But are any of them weary of it?" asked God.

And they all looked at Him and became silent.

"None are as weary" said the Vicar, "as the Vixen I saw."

"How did you know it was a Vixen?" asked the Poacher.

"I examined her closely," said the Vicar. "And I was able to do that because she'd been wearied to death."

And he went on:

An October robin kept
Stringing its song
On gossamer that snapped.
The weir-pool hung
Lit with honey leaves.
Ploughed hills crisp as loaves

In the high morning.
I waded the river's way
Body and ear leaning
For whatever the world might say
Of the word in her womb
Curled unborn and dumb.

Still as the heron
I let the world grow near
With a ghostly salmon
Hanging in thin air
So real it was holy
And watching seemed to kneel.

And there I saw the vixen
Coiled on her bank porch.
Her paws were bloody sticks.
Ears on guard for her searchers
She had risked a sleep
And misjudged how deep.

90

Everybody was silent, thinking about the Vicar's Vixen,
when suddenly the Farmer burst into song:

O he steals our crooked speeches, says the Hunting Horn,
    Steals our slanders and our lies
    Which are demons in disguise,
And he nails them to his tongue, so it hangs out pink and long,
And he flees us like a robber, says the Hunting Horn.

And he steals out of our souls all the popping fiery coals
    Our malice and suspicion
    Which are devils in perdition,
And he nails them to his ears, where they can't be quenched by tears,
And he flees us like a robber, says the Hunting Horn.

And he steals out of our throats the greediness that gloats
    On the muttons, beefs and porks
    That weep upon our forks,
And he nails it in his grin, where the wind blows out and in,
And he flees us like a robber, says the Hunting Horn.

And he steals our wicked blood and he rides it through the mud,
    The mare of blood that bears us,
    The red hunter that wears us,
And it's like a witch's stick that he rides through thin and thick
As he flees us like a robber, says the Hunting Horn.

92

And he's nailed our fear of darkness to his four paws dipped in quickness,
>   Our cowardice a nail
>   In the white tip of his tail,
With the limestone from our hearts, he's whitewashed his underparts,
And he flees us like a robber, says the Hunting Horn.

Then in a belling applause of hounds, he bounds off the earth and leaves no traces—
Just as if we'd washed our hands and faces.

Now it was God's turn to look alarmed. But only for a moment. Then He gazed at the Farmer, with his hands on his knees, as if He were remembering something far off, till finally He said:

"Why is it that all these creatures have such a hard time?"

"Is man any better off?" asked the Schoolteacher.

"Man is a worm," said the Shepherd, out of his sleep.

"A worm?" cried the Farmer. "I sometimes wish I was a worm." And he went on:

I hear for every acre there's a ton of worms beneath.
I hear that worm-meat's better meat than fatted barley beef.
We're farming only half our farms, and that's the new belief.

I think I'm growing barley, bullocks, pigs and lambs galore.
From six a.m. till nine at night I toil my body sore.
But I'm only feeding the roots of the worms, it's worms I'm working for.

Below my clover meadows worms are bellowing in the dark.
They're bound for nobody's oven, one or two might go to the lark.
They gobble their way through the earth's black pudding safe as they were in the ark.

Worms riot and revel in their rude and naked hordes.
And most of what I fatten, far, far more than my farm affords
Falls into their idle mouths, and the whole lot live like lords.

"According to the theory of evolution," said the School-
teacher, "Man was formerly a reptile."
"Like a weasel," said the Poacher. "A weasel is a reptile."
"How?" asked God in surprise.
"To begin with," the Poacher said:

Its face is a furry lizard's face, but prettier.

Only the Weasel
Is wick as a weasel.
Whipping whisk

Of a grim cook. And a lit trail
Of gunpowder, he fizzes
Toward a shocking stop.

His tail jaunts along for the laughs.

His grandfather, to keep him active,
Buried the family jewels
Under some rabbit's ear.

Tyrannosaur—miniaturized
To slip through every loop-hole
In the laws of rats and mice.

Terrorist
Of the eggs—

Over the rim of the thrush's nest
The Weasel's face, bright as the Evening Star,
Brings night.

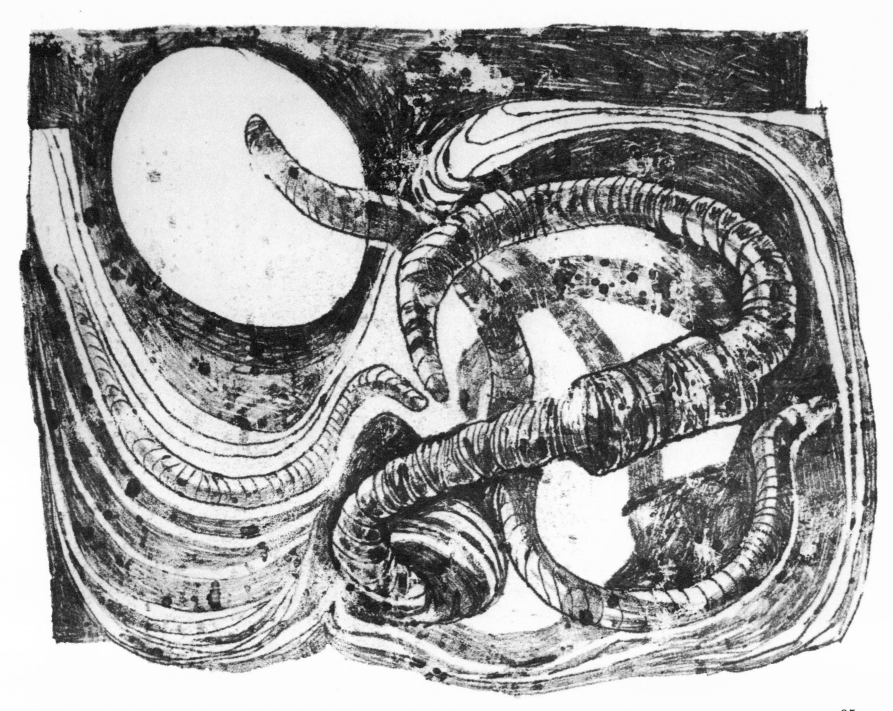

"But first," said the Vicar, "it brings who?"
And he answered his own question, saying:

To see the twilight white Owl wavering over the dew-mist
Startles my heart, a mouse in its house, remembering a dim past

When we were only the weight of shrews, maybe, and everything ate us
In a steaming, echoing jungle of night-flying alligators,

And the dawn-chorus shook the swamps, a booming orchestra
Where Brontosaurs were merely the flutes, and land-whales beat
                                        on the drum of the ear—

It has all sunk into the fern-fringed forest pool of the Owl's eye,
But it reaches over the farm like a claw in the Owl's catspaw cry.

The Owl sways, weighing the hushed world, his huge gaze dry and light
As a blown dandelion clock, or the moon-husk of the oldest night.

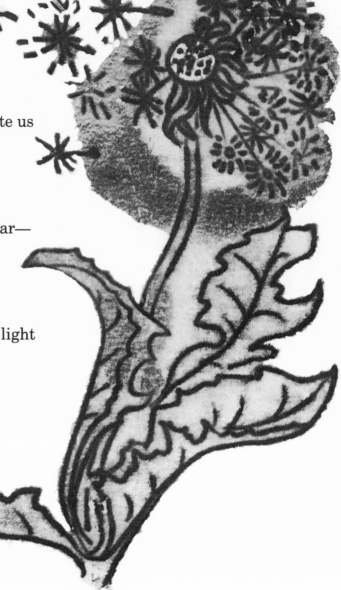

"My favourite thing about night" said the Farmer's son, "is catching carp."
"A fish!" said God's Son, interested.
And the Farmer's son went on:

When the heat-wave world of midsummer
Is set out to cool, in the oven mouth,
After sundown,

The pond
Wobbles, as if the bed of it, at one corner
Were still on a red ring.

Bats shiver. The western sky
Cools its powdery crucible colours.
It's a midsummer madness. Crouching

To catch a great carp is how I imagine
Gold-fever. And right at your feet, maybe,
Earth will suddenly open—

A bullion chest will heave up
Streaming with lilies, and roll over
And you'll grab at it—
Maybe you'll glimpse a spill of doubloons
As it slides under again, too heavy.

Then the pond weltering. The first star
Molten and writhing.
                              And you're left

Silver-plated

A glistening piece of the treasure

As the moon climbs up your back.

The Vicar was singing again, and the Farmer's wife looked at him in alarm. Perhaps the nearness of God and his Son had made the man slightly tipsy. She had never guessed he could sing with such gusto.

The Hedgehog has Itchy the Hedgehog to hug
And a hedgehog bug has a hedgehog bug.

Hedgehog with hedgehog is happy at ease
And hedgehogs with fleas, and fleas with fleas.

The batch of the Flea's eggs hatch in the crutch
Of the Hedgehog's armpit, a hot rich hutch.

The Hedgehog's clutch of hoglets come
In the niche of a ditch, from the Hedgepig's tum.

And so they enjoy their mutual joke
With a pricklety itch and a scratchety poke.

"You see," said God to his Son, "these creatures are their toys. Some they keep, some they break. How many escape unbroken? Not even the swiftest."
"The Hare" said the Poacher, "is the swiftest."
"Who knows the Truth of it?" asked God's Son. His eyes were resting on the Farmer's daughter as he spoke, and she looked startled, a little like a hare for a moment, before she said:

That Elf
Riding his awkward pair of haunchy legs

That weird long-eared Elf
Wobbling down the highway

Don't overtake him, don't try to drive past him,
He's scatty, he's all over the road,
He can't keep his steering, in his ramshackle go-cart,
His big loose wheels, buckled and rusty,
Nearly wobbling off

And all the screws in his head wobbling and loose

And his eyes wobbling

    "What is a Hare?" asked God, looking now at the Vicar.

The Hare is a very fragile thing.
The life in the hare is a glassy goblet, and her yellow-fringed
                   frost-flake belly says: Fragile.

The hare's bones are light glass. And the hare's face—

Who lifted her face to the Lord?
Her new-budded nostrils and lips,
For the daintiest pencillings, the last eyelash touches

Delicate as the down of a moth,
And the breath of awe
Which fixed the mad beauty-light
In her look
As if her retina
Were a moon perpetually at full.

Who is it, at midnight on the A30,
The Druid soul,
The night-streaker, the sudden lumpy goblin
That thumps the car under the belly
Then cries with human pain
And becomes a human baby on the road
That you dare hardly pick up?

Or leaps, like a long bat with little headlights,
Straight out of darkness
Into the driver's nerves
With a jangle of cries
As if the car had crashed into a flying harp

So that the driver's nerves flail and cry
Like a burst harp.

101

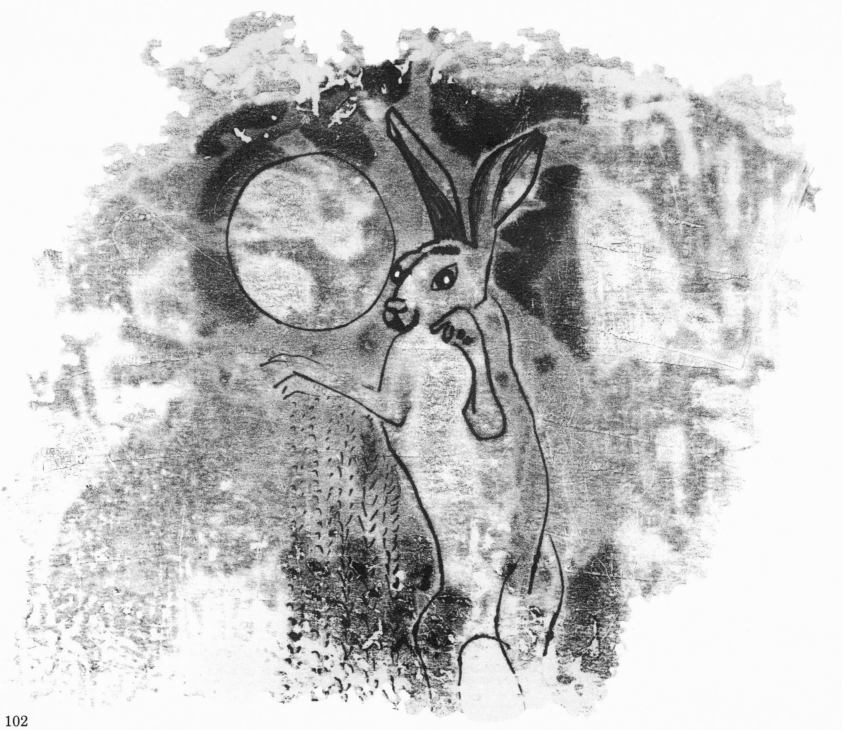

"And now you," said God to the Poacher. "What have you to say?"

"About the Hare?" asked the Poacher anxiously. He wondered if God knew everything. He supposed He did.

"The Truth," said God's Son.

"Tell us about those times you lie there," said the Vicar, "soaked with dew, in the early dawn, with your cold gun. And a hare happens along that way."

"Why, Vicar," said the Poacher, "it's a wonderful sight."

Uneasy she nears
As if she were being lured, but fearful,
Nearer.
Like a large egg toppling itself—mysterious!

Then she'll stretch, tall, on her hind feet,
And lean on the air,
Taut—like a stilled yacht waiting on the air—

And what does the hunter see? A fairy woman?
A dream beast?
A kangaroo of the March corn?

The loveliest face listening,
Her black-tipped ears hearing the bud of the blackthorn
Opening its lips,
Her black-tipped hairs hearing tomorrow's weather
Combing the mare's tails,
Her snow-fluff belly feeling for the first breath,
Her orange nape, foxy with its dreams of the fox—

Witch-maiden
Heavy with trembling blood—astounding
How much blood there is in her body!
She is a moony pond of quaking blood

Twitched with spells, her gold-ringed eye spellbound—

Carrying herself so gently, balancing
Herself with the gentlest touches
As if her eyes brimmed—

"More, more!" cried God's Son.
And God looked at the Schoolteacher.
"I've seen her," said the Schoolteacher,

I've seen her,
A lank, lean hare, with her long thin feet
And her long, hollow thighs,
And her ears like ribbons
Careering by moonlight
In her Flamenco, her heels flinging the dust
On the drum of the hill.

And I've seen him, hobbling stiffly
God of Leapers
Surprised by dawn, earth-bound, and stained
With drying mud,
Painfully rocking over the furrows

With his Leaping-Legs, his Power-Thighs
Much too powerful for ordinary walking,
So powerful
They seem almost a burden, almost a problem,
Nearly an aching difficulty for him
When he tries to loiter or pause,
Nearly a heaving pain to lift and move
Like turning a cold car-engine with a bent crank handle—

Till a shock, a terror, with a bang
Grabs at her ears. An oven door
Bangs open, both barrels, and a barking
Bursts out of onions—
                              and she leaps
And her heels
Hard as angle-iron kick salt and pepper
Into the lurcher's eyes—
                              and kick and kick
The spinning, turnip world
Into the lurcher's gullet—
                              as she slips
Between thin hawthorn and thinner bramble
Into tomorrow.

Then God looked at the Farmer. But the Farmer's
conscience was clear. And he began:

There's something eerie about a hare, no matter how stringy and old.
I heard of a hare caught in a snowdrift, brought in under a coat from the cold
Turned by firelight into a tall fine woman who many a strange tale told.

The hare has a powerful whiff with her, even when she's a pet.
Her back as broad and strong as a dog, and her kick like a bull-calf, yet
Into your dreams she waltzes strung with starlight and music, a marionette.

They say it's a nude witch dancing her rings though it looks like a lolloping hare
Circling the farm, like a full moon circling the globe, and leaning to stare
Huge-eyed in at the midnight window down at the sleeping children there.

Something scares me about a hare, like seeing an escapee
From a looney-bin, lurching and loping along in his flapping pyjamas, free—
Or meeting a woman mad with religion who has fastened her eyes on me.

You'll never hurt a hare after you've heard her cry in pain.
A mother's scream, a baby's scream, and a needle slips in through your ear and brain.
To prick and prick your heart when you even hear of the hurt of a hare again.

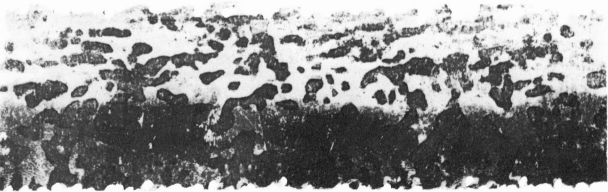

106

God and his Son sat looking at the softly glowing souls of the people lying there on the grass. They were all thinking about the Hare.

"Let's get on to magpies," said the Poacher. "They're quite moonlike, in their way."

"Egg-eaters!" said the Vicar sharply.

"Protectors of the orchard," said the Farmer.

"It depends" said the Farmer's daughter, "which you prefer to see on the twigs: bullfinches or apples. You have a choice." And she began:

A mournful note, a crying note
A single tin-whistle half-note, insistent
Echoed by another
Slightly bluer with a brief distance
In March, in the draughty, dripping orchard.

And again and again—and the echo prompt.
Bullfinch is melancholy.

Bullfinch wants us to feel a cold air, a shivery sadness
And to pity him in his need,
In the poverty start of the year, the hungry end,
Too early
In his Persian plum-plush wedding regalia
Above bleak, virginal daffodils.

He wants us to feel protective
At least for as long as it takes him
To strip every tree of its bud-blossom—

To pack a summerful of apple-power
Under his flaming shirt.

"What about Roger in all this?" the Farmer's wife asked suddenly. And she went straight on:

Asleep he wheezes at his ease.
He only wakes to scratch his fleas.

He hogs the fire, he bakes his head
As if it were a loaf of bread.

He's just a sack of snoring dog.
You can lug him like a log.

You can roll him with your foot.
He'll stay snoring where he's put.

Take him out for exercise
He'll roll in cowclap up to his eyes.

He will not race, he will not romp.
He saves his strength for gobble and chomp.

He'll work as hard as you could wish
Emptying the dinner dish,

Then flops flat, and digs down deep,
Like a miner, into sleep.

"He probably has dreams about a diamond, if he sleeps like a miner," said the Farmer. "I dig my way through the muck, and I had a dream about a pheasant."
"A dream—" cried God's Son. "I have dreams!"
But the Farmer went on:

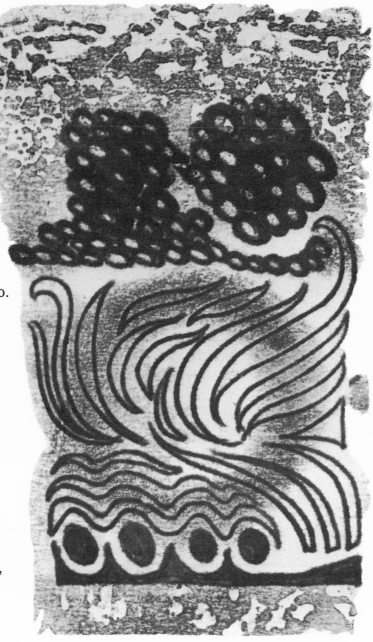

I was carrying our cat.
Across a ploughed field. Above us, a blue-black piled-up sky
Boiled bulgy clouds.
I thought: it's like giant blackberries. And I thought:
If it rains, I'll be a queer colour.

There came a crack of lightning.
It was like being cracked over the skull with a splintering bamboo.
The lid flew off everything. I saw the blue-hot centre.
I thought: This is it, a planet's crashed into us.
And our cat was so scared, it peed all warm down my shirt.

Then everything was alright again.
Except our cat had turned into some kind of bird
That started struggling to fly. I had to hold it hard.
The thing about this bird
Was it was made of gold.

All soft warm scale-armour, its feathers were scales
And every scale was the flame of a candle
Hammered out flat—part solid, but the gold fringe still soft flame,
And I knew these flames were off candles
That angels had held. Suddenly this bird

Burst free and bounced on to the tilth in front of me
And stood there, dishevelled.
Then it shook its flames into shape, it whirled itself
Like a bottleful of bright coins, and stood brighter.
It had horns on its head. And I saw its head

Was a word in Chinese.
I stared into its flame, I couldn't stare into it
                                        hard enough.

And I stared at its head—
I knew that word had a meaning
But the meaning was too big, I had to hold my head in

Because I could feel it trying to split.
It was a funny dream all right.
Then my head actually split—the two halves came
                                        right apart
And the bird was looking at me, I saw its barbed tongue
And it let out a yell, and I woke up—

What I'd heard was a pheasant.

 "I had a dream" said the Vicar, "about a dog."
 "Tell us," said God's Son, "and I'll interpret it."
 The Vicar seemed unsure whether he ought to tell this
dream or not.
 But finally he began:

I dreamed I woke and was a bark
Working at the postman and the boy
With the newspaper. I watched hard
My master's breakfast mouth,
Sitting with all my might.
With all my skill I caught
The bacon-rind and did for it—
Clapping my chops to make a neat job.
When he stood I was so quick
Already standing, and my tail turning over
Without a problem. On the way
I checked every sniff—Good morning! Good morning!
I even managed a handy bark
At the dog on the next farm, over four fields
And got a good boy for it.
Cows' heels were just starters warming me up—
I could do it with my tongue idling.
Serious at sheep was how I earned my keep
Working my master's face
Through all its shapes, without a mistake,
Getting his arms right each time
And making his whistle easy.
My ears fairly ached
At stopping and starting.
I had every single mutton helpless
Under my ideas.
I threw in a few dodges—
Spinning them on one hoof,
Rolling the flock up on three sides at once
Like a pasty,
Pouring them through a nozzle.

I made a point
Of snatching a good boy
From under the tail of each one.
My panting
Finally used all the work up,
And daylight had to go.
I ate a bowl of good boy
Still keeping my master's eyes safe,
And resting his footsteps in my right ear
Till I slept.
Believe me, I slept without a pause
Even when the sleep-wolf
Jeering at me, dashed through my skin
Like a clock-alarm.

"One more," said God.
"A long one," cried God's Son. "Let it be a long one. About a
fish. Or about a badger maybe. Or a mole. No news of the Mole.
And what about the Mighty Ant? And where's the Cat?
Where's the Crow?"
Nobody spoke.
"What about a fox?" said God's Son, hopefully.
"I once met a fox," said the Schoolteacher.
"Tell us," cried God's Son.
"It was the end of the year," said the Schoolteacher. "A mild,
misty sort of day."

Drip-tree stillness. And a spring-feeling elation
Of mid-morning oxygen. There was a yeasty simmering
Over the land—all compass points were trembling
Bristling with starlings, hordes out of the North,
Bubbly and hopeful.

We stood in the mist-rawness
Of the sodden earth. The Day Before Christmas.
We could hear the grass seeping.

Then a wraith-smoke
Writhed up from a far field and condensed
On a frieze of dwarfish hedge-oaks—sizzling
Like power-pylons in mist.
We eased our way into the landscape.
Casual midnightish draughts, in the soaking stillness.
Itch of starlings was everywhere.
                                        Our gun
Was old, rust-ugly, single-barrelled, borrowed
For a taste of English sport. My friend had come
From eighteen years' Australian estrangement
Twelve thousand miles through thin air
To walk again on the tight hills of the West,
In the ruby and emerald glow, the leaf-wet oils
Of his memory's masterpiece.
                                        Hedge-sparrows
Needled the bramble-mass undergrowth
With their weepy warnings.
                                        He had the gun.

113

We hardened our eyes. A patrol.
The gun-muzzle was sniffing. And the broad land
Tautened into wider, nervier contrasts
Of living and unliving. Our eyes feathered over it—
It was a touchy detonator. Slow,

Bootprints between the ranks of baby barley
Heel and toe we trod
Narrowed behind the broad gaze of the gun
Down the long woodside. I was the dog.

Now I got into the wood. I pushed parallel
And slightly ahead—the idea
Was to flush something for the gun's amusement.

I go delicate. I don't want to panic
My listeners into a crouch-freeze.
I want them to keep their initiative
And slip away, confident, still careless,
Out across the gun.
                                        Pigeons, too far,
Burst up from under the touch
Of our furthest listenings. A bramble
Claws across my knee, and a blackbird
Five yards off explodes its booby-trap
Shattering wetly
Black and yellow alarm-dazzlings, and a long string
Of fireworks down the wood. It settles
To a hacking chatter and that blade-ringing
Like a flint on an axe-head.

I wait.
That startled me too.
I know I am a Gulliver now
Tied by my every slightest move
To a thousand fears. But I move—
And a jay, invisibly somewhere safe
Starts pretending to tear itself in half
From the mouth backwards. With three screams
It scares itself to silence.
                                        The whole wood
Has hidden in the wood. Its mossy tunnels
Seem to age as I listen. A raven
Dabs a single charcoal toad-croak
Into the finished picture.
                                        I come out
To join my friend in the field. We need a new plan
To surprise something.
                                        But as I come over the wire
He is pointing, silent.
I look. One hundred yards
Down the woodside, somebody
Is watching us.

A strangely dark fox
Motionless in his robe of office
Is watching us. It is a shock.

Too deep in the magic wood, suddenly
We have met the magician.

Then he's away—
A slender figurine, dark and witchy,
A rocking nose-down lollop, and the load of tail
Floating behind him, over the swell of faint corn
Into the long arm of woodland opposite.

The gun does nothing. But we gaze after
Like men who have been given a secret sign.
We are studying the changed expression
Of that straggle of scrub and poor trees
Which is now the disguise of a fox.

And the gun is thinking. The gun
Is working its hunter's magic.
It is transforming us, there in the dull mist,
To two suits of cold armour—
Empty of all but a strange new humming,
A mosquito of primaeval excitements.

And as we start to walk out over the field
The gun smiles.

The fox will be under brambles.
He has set up his antennae,
His dials are glowing and quivering,
Every hair adjusts itself
To our coming.

Will he wait in the copse
Till we've made our move, as if this were a game
He is interested to play?
Or has he gone through and away over further fields?
Or down and into the blueish mass and secrecy
Of the main wood?

Under a fat oak, where the sparse copse
Joins the main wood, my friend leans in ambush.
Well out in the corn, talking to air
Like quiet cogs, I stroll to the top of the strip—
Pretending to be both of us—
Then pierce the brush, clumsy as a bullock, a trampling
Like purposeless machinery, towards my friend,
Noisy enough for him to know
Where not to point his blind gun.

Somewhere between us
The fox is inspecting me, magnified.
And now I tangle all his fears with a silence,
Then a sudden abrupt advance, then again silence,
Then a random change of direction—

And almost immediately,
Almost before I've decided we are serious—
The blast wall hits me, the gun bang bursts
Like a paper bag in my face,
The whole day bursts like a paper bag—

But a new world is created instantly
With no visible change.

I pause. I call. My friend does not answer
Everything is just as it had been.
The corroded blackberry leaves,
The crooked naked trees, fingering sky
Are all the usual, careful shapes
Of the usual silence.
I go forward. And now I see my friend
As if he had missed,
Leaning against his tree, casual.

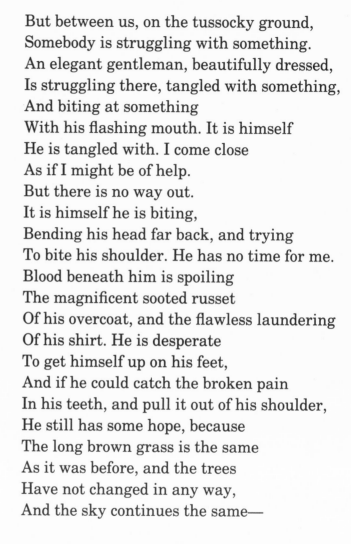

But between us, on the tussocky ground,
Somebody is struggling with something.
An elegant gentleman, beautifully dressed,
Is struggling there, tangled with something,
And biting at something
With his flashing mouth. It is himself
He is tangled with. I come close
As if I might be of help.
But there is no way out.
It is himself he is biting,
Bending his head far back, and trying
To bite his shoulder. He has no time for me.
Blood beneath him is spoiling
The magnificent sooted russet
Of his overcoat, and the flawless laundering
Of his shirt. He is desperate
To get himself up on his feet,
And if he could catch the broken pain
In his teeth, and pull it out of his shoulder,
He still has some hope, because
The long brown grass is the same
As it was before, and the trees
Have not changed in any way,
And the sky continues the same—

It is doing the impossible deliberately
To set the gun-muzzle at his chest
And funnel that sky-bursting bang
Through a sudden blue-pit in his fur
Into the earth beneath him.

He cannot believe it has happened.

His chin sinks forward, and he half-closes his mouth
In a smile
Of incredulous bitterness,
And half-closes his eyes
Into a fineness beyond pain—

And it is a dead fox in the dank woodland.

And I stand awake—as one wakes
From what feels like a cracking blow on the head.

That second shot has ruined his skin.
We chop his tail off
Thick and long as a forearm, and black.
Then bundle him and his velvet legs
His bag of useless jewels,
The phenomenal technology inside his head,
Into a hole, under a bulldozed stump,
Like picnic rubbish. There the memory ends.

We must have walked away.

Everybody was silent.
Suddenly—a shocking noise. For a terrible moment the
Farmer's daughter thought her donkey had come quietly up
the hill, and was now trying to laugh at them all.
Then they all realized it was the Shepherd. He was singing.
With his eyes closed, he was singing:

O early one dawn I walked over the dew
And I saw a strange thing I will now tell to you.

Where mud had been trampled at a trough by the cattle
Till it looked like the field of the famous Somme battle

I saw two bare creatures, stark naked were they
Full length in the mud, at the dawn of the day.

They were big blue-nosed lobworms who stretched to embrace
From their separate dug-outs, in that dreadful place.

O they twisted together like two loving tongues
And they had not a care for the world and its wrongs.

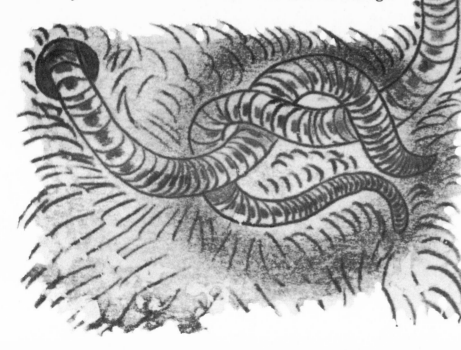

O they clung in a spittle, like passionate lips
From their separate holes, as from separate ships.

And that was a wonder to watch in the dawn
In the world wet with dew, like a garden new-born.

It was Adam and Eve in the earliest light—
And I was like Satan, for they suddenly took fright.

Their loving was chilled at the touch of my stare—
O I almost could hear it, their cry of despair

As like snapping elastic, they whipped back apart
And I can still feel it, the shock and the smart

As they vanished in earth, each alone to its den.
And I've never seen such a marvel again.

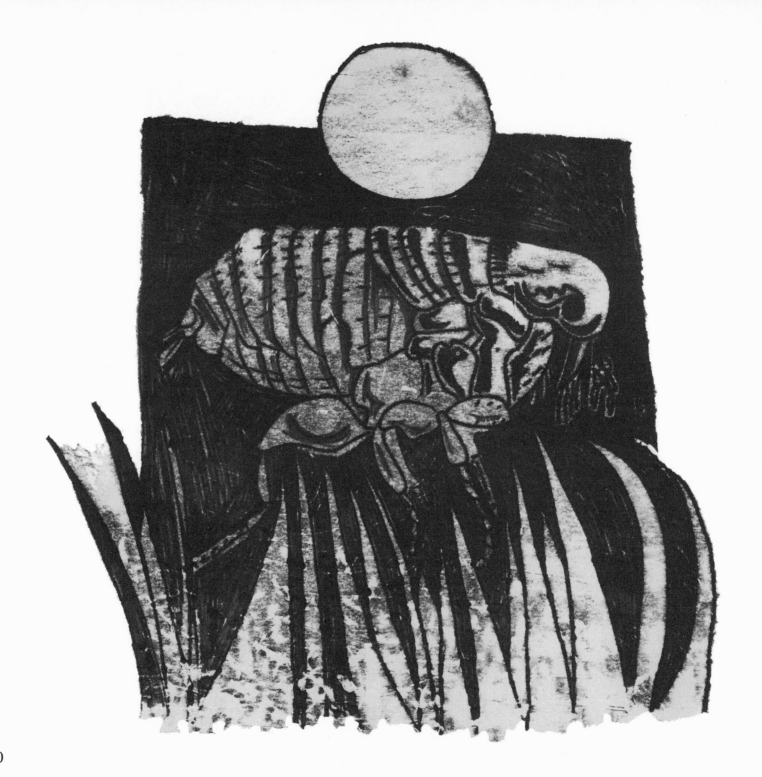

"Enough!" said God. "Enough. We have heard enough."

"But have we heard the Truth?" asked God's Son. He still had no idea what the Truth might be.

"No, not the Truth," said God sadly. "Not the Truth."

"Then tell us the Truth," said God's Son. "What is the Truth?"

All the misty glowing shapes of the people on the grass were watching God, whose face now seemed brighter than ever.

"What is the Truth?" cried God's Son, insistent.

"The Truth" said God finally, "is this. The Truth is that I was those Worms."

God's Son stared at his Father, looking blank.

"And the Truth is" God went on, "that I was that Fox. Just as I was that Foal. As I am, I am. I am that Foal. And I am the Cow. I am the Weasel and the Mouse. The Wood Pigeon and the Partridge. The Goat, the Badger, the Hedgehog, the Hare. Yes, and the Hedgehog's Flea. I am each of these things. The Rat. The Fly. And each of these things is Me. It is. It is. That is the Truth."

I AM THE RAT

I AM THE CAT

I AM THE FOX

I AM THE GOAT

I AM THE BADGER

AND THE HARE

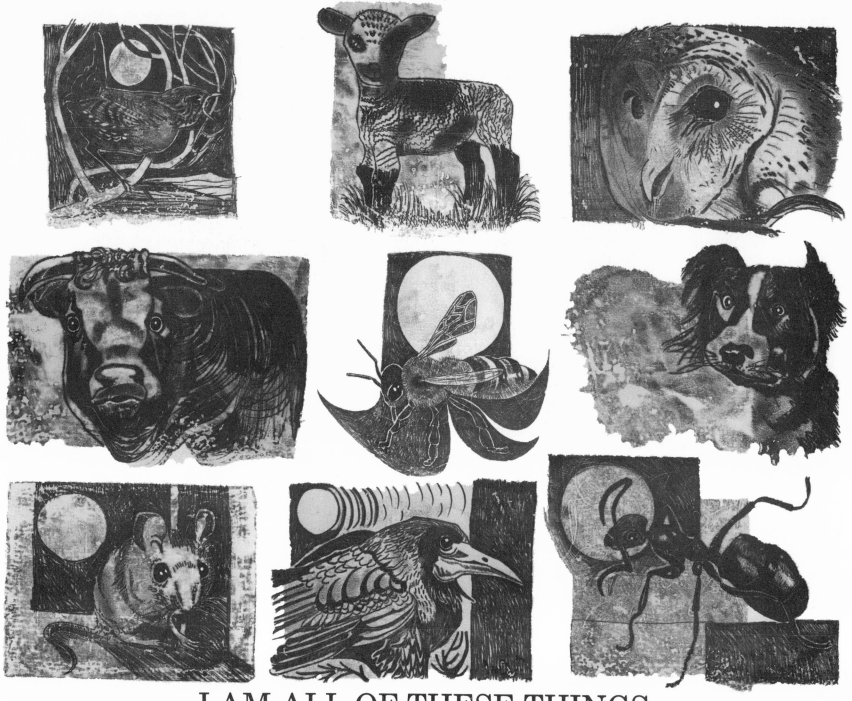

I AM ALL OF THESE THINGS

God's Son remembered all that had been said about these creatures, and He stared at the misty shapes of the souls on the grass, and under his gaze the shapes began to fade.

"Don't go away," cried God's Son. "Stay a moment. Did you hear all that? Did you know the Truth about all these creatures?"

But as He spoke they thinned, until they were no more than faint wraiths of mist creeping along the hillsides. And God's Son saw the oak leaves move, and felt on his cheek a slight chill of air.

He turned and saw that his Father had disappeared. Instead, the sky was very bright under a long low cloud in the east. And the middle of that cloud glowed like the gilded lintel of a doorway that had been rubbed bright.

Then God's Son hesitated. It occurred to him, with a little shiver, that He was where He had wanted to be. He stood on the earth. And below him He could see the roofs of the farm. And there in the early mist was the village, and beyond it, in every direction, other farms, where the people still slept, but where the cocks were already beginning to crow.

St. Columba's High School,
Dunfermline.